MADE IN
ANCIENT EGYPT

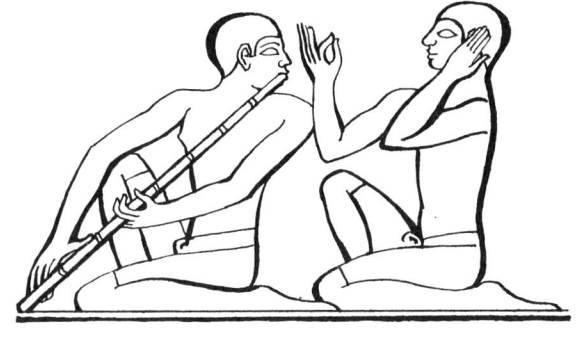

MADE IN
ANCIENT EGYPT

by Christine Price

Illustrated with photographs and drawings

NEW YORK

E. P. DUTTON & CO., INC.

ALSO BY CHRISTINE PRICE

Made in the Middle Ages
Made in the Renaissance
The Story of Moslem Art
Made in Ancient Greece

Published simultaneously in Canada by
Clarke, Irwin & Company Limited, Toronto and Vancouver

Library of Congress Catalog Card Number: 73–78946

Lithographed by The Murray Printing Company

SBN 0-525-34308-3 (Trade)   SBN 0-525-34309-1 (DLLB)

For
Claudia Lyon

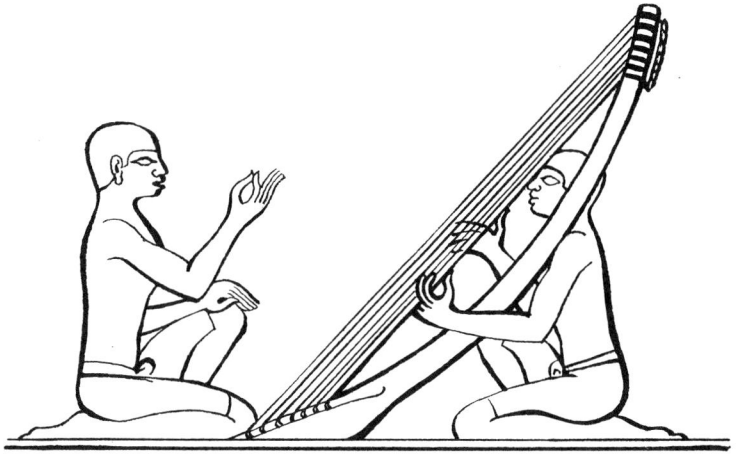

Contents

Author's Note		8
Time Chart and Map	*preceding*	9

I   The People of the Two Lands

Temples and Tombs	10
The River	16
Kings, Gods, and Animals	25

II   The Age of the Pyramid Builders

"Staircase to Heaven"	34
The Pyramid Builders	40
All the Good Things of Life	52
Men and Women Great and Small	58

III   The Two Lands Reunited

    Sculpture and the New Spirit   64

    The Art of the Painter   70

    Jewels for Princesses   79

IV   Thebes and the Age of Empire

    "Splendid Are the Splendors of Amon" 85

    Famous Men of Thebes   93

    The Southern Sanctuary   105

V   Akhenaten's Revolution

    New Art at the King's Command   113

    Treasures of the Young King   120

VI   The Victorious Pharaohs

    The Walls of Karnak   128

    To the Glory of Ramesses   133

    Servants in the Place of Truth   144

    The Enduring Art of Egypt   152

    List of Illustrations   154

    Books for Further Reading   160

Author's Note

I am very grateful to the following for providing me with photographs and permitting me to include them in my book:

The Trustees of the British Museum, London; the Brooklyn Museum, New York; the Egyptian Museum, Cairo; the Metropolitan Museum of Art, New York; the Museum of Fine Arts, Boston; the Oriental Institute of the University of Chicago; the Royal Scottish Museum, Edinburgh; the Center of Documentation and Studies of Ancient Egypt, Cairo; Lehnert and Landrock, Cairo; the United Arab Republic Tourist and Information Center, New York; and the Art Reference Bureau, Ancram, New York.

I would like to thank all those who have helped with my work on this book and generously shared with me their knowledge of Egyptian art and history, particulary Dr. Charles F. Nims, who extended to me the hospitality of Chicago House at Luxor and showed me the glories of ancient Thebes; and Dr. Labib Habachi, who was most helpful and encouraging during my stay in Egypt.

My grateful thanks are also due to Miss Nora Scott and to Dr. Nims for reading and criticizing my manuscript.

As I have tried to keep the text free of dates, the approximate dates of the Egyptian dynasties are listed at the beginning, based upon the chronology of the British Museum, *Introductory Guide to the Egyptian Collections*. At the end is a list of recent books on ancient Egypt. Most of them are richly illustrated and all are exciting reading.

My book is meant to be only a gateway to the wonders of ancient Egyptian art, and I hope that some readers who pass through it will set out from there on their own voyages of discovery.

C. P.

Time Chart
and Map

The Dynasties of Ancient Egypt

(Historical periods covered by the six parts of this book with
their approximate dates and some of the principal rulers)

I
THE PEOPLE
OF THE
TWO LANDS
	ARCHAIC PERIOD
	
	I Dynasty 3100–2890 B.C.
	    Narmer
	    Uadji
	
	II Dynasty 2890–2686 B.C.
	    Khasekhem

II
THE AGE
OF THE
PYRAMID
BUILDERS
	OLD KINGDOM
	
	III Dynasty 2686–2613 B.C.
	    Zoser
	
	IV Dynasty 2613–2494 B.C.
	    Khufu
	    Khafre
	    Menkaure
	
	V Dynasty 2494–2345 B.C.
	
	VI Dynasty 2345–2181 B.C.
	
	FIRST INTERMEDIATE PERIOD (*VII–X Dynasties*)

MIDDLE KINGDOM III

XI Dynasty 2133–1991 B.C. THE

Mentuhotep II (2060–2010 B.C.) TWO LANDS

REUNITED

XII Dynasty 1991–1786 B.C.

Senwosret II (1897–1878 B.C.)

Senwosret III (1878–1843 B.C.)

XIII Dynasty 1786–1633 B.C.

SECOND INTERMEDIATE PERIOD *(XIV–XVII Dynasties)*

NEW KINGDOM IV

XVIII Dynasty 1567–1320 B.C. THEBES AND

Hatshepsut (1503–1482 B.C) THE AGE

Thutmose III (1504–1450 B.C.) OF EMPIRE

Amenhotep III (1417–1379 B.C.)

Amenhotep IV—Akhenaten (1379–1362 B.C.) V

Tutankhamen (1361–1352 B.C.) AKHENATEN'S

REVOLUTION

XIX Dynasty 1320–1200 B.C.

Seti I (1318–1304 B.C.)

Ramesses II (1304–1237 B.C.) VI

THE

XX Dynasty 1200–1085 B.C. VICTORIOUS

Ramesses III (1196–1166 B.C.) PHARAOHS

LATER DYNASTIES *(XXI–XXX)* 1085–343 B.C.

(Conquest of Egypt by Alexander the Great 332 B.C.)

MEDITERRANEAN SEA

CYPRUS

SYRIA

R. Orontes

Kadesh

Byblos
Beirut
Sidon
Tyre

Damascus

PALESTINE

Jerusalem

Tanis

LIBYAN
DESERT

Giza
Sakkara
Dahshur
Meidum

Cairo
Memphis

SINAI

ARABIA

Lahun

Beni Hasan
Hermopolis
Amarna

River Nile

Abydos
Deir el Bahri
Medinet Habu

Koptos
Luxor
(Thebes)

Kosseir

RED SEA

Aswan

First
Cataract

Abu Simbel

EGYPT
and the
Ancient
Near East

1 The People of the Two Lands

Temples and Tombs

For more than four thousand years the Pyramids of Giza have stood at the desert's edge. They rise above the green valley of the Nile like three mountain peaks, pale desert-brown under the hot blue sky of noon, black against the fires of the sunset. The pyramids seem to be a part of the land, solid and lasting as the rock of their foundation. The Sphinx that lies before them is carved from that rock, a powerful image of a lion with the head of a king.

The pyramids, the tombs of three great kings, have become the symbols of the enduring kingdom of ancient Egypt. When the pyramids had stood for a thousand years, the Egyptians

Above THE GREAT SPHINX, GIZA

were still erecting mighty monuments. They built huge temples
up the river valley, with columned halls and courtyards so
colossal that men moved in them like ants. Strange gods were

11

TEMPLE OF AMON
AT KARNAK

worshiped in the sanctuaries and pictured on the walls, and in the temple courts were the statues of kings—rigid seated figures and standing giants with fists clenched at their sides.

Travelers to Egypt, since the time of the ancient Greeks, have gazed in wonder and bewilderment at the pyramids, the Sphinx, and the temples of the Nile valley. Surely the Egyptian builders had some secret knowledge denied to other men!

12

How could the stones of the pyramids be moved by human strength? What was the meaning of the mysterious writings on the temple walls?

The towns of the ancient Egyptians, built of mud-brick, wood, and plaster, were destroyed through the centuries or left to crumble away. Only the temples and tombs remained, built of lasting stone or carved from the harsh cliffs along the desert's edge, and it seemed to men of later ages that the ancient Egyptians had devoted their whole lives to religion and to elaborate preparations for death. Their art was solemn and filled with mystery because they were a solemn and mysterious people.

Yet how can we fit into this picture some of the things that have been found in the tombs and temples?

In a tomb we can see a carving of dancers, kicking high to the rhythm of clapping hands; and in another tomb, a painting of a feast or of a duck hunt in the marshes. Among the treasures buried with the dead were exquisite jewelry, small figures glazed in brilliant blue, and furniture plated with gold.

DANCERS
IN A TOMB
AT SAKKARA

BATTLE SCENE
AT KARNAK

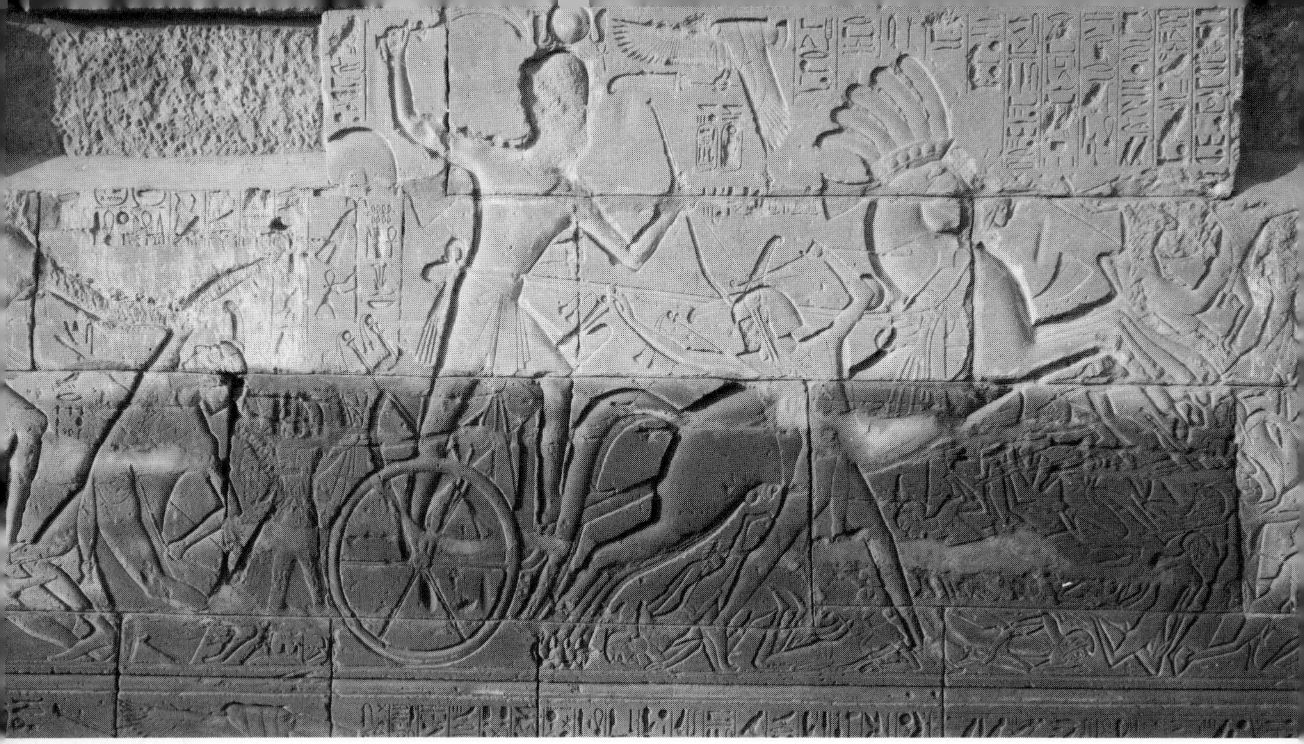

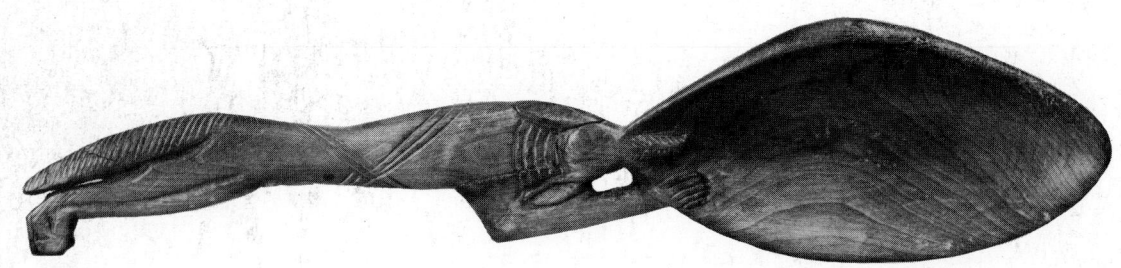

On the walls of a temple Egyptian sculptors carved a splendid scene of victory in battle, alive with prancing horses and struggling men. A craftsman could turn a common ointment jar into a thing of beauty, or whittle a wooden spoon in the shape of an animal. Manuscripts, written on long scrolls, were illustrated with fine colored drawings, and when one artist drew a lion playing draughts and a cat driving a flock of geese, we may even suspect he had a sense of humor!

The task of the Egyptian artist, whether he worked with paint or stone, wood or metal, was to make the things that

WOODEN SPOON IN THE FORM OF A JACKAL AND SHELL

PENDANT OF INLAID GOLD

people ordered from him. If much of his finest work has been found in tombs, this is not because his employers were oppressed by thoughts of death. For them, death was not to be feared but to be conquered.

The Egyptians loved life. They wanted to enjoy forever the life they knew in the valley of the Nile, where the waters of the great river ruled their days, molded their thought, and made them what they were.

PAPYRUS SCROLL
WITH ANIMAL
DRAWINGS

Among the thickets of bright green papyrus plants that fringed the Nile, the people fished and hunted from small boats made of bundles of papyrus stems. Thousands of waterfowl flew up before the hunters with a sunlit flashing of wings —duck and heron and Egyptian geese, graceful egrets and the black-and-white sacred ibis. The river teemed with fish, crocodiles basked on the mudbanks, and it was great sport to harpoon the hippopotamus that wallowed in the water through the long day's heat.

The river ruled the lives of all who lived along it. Like the birds and beasts and fish, the Egyptians were governed by the movement of the waters. Each summer they watched the river rise until the whole valley was flooded to the desert hills. In autumn, when the water drained away, it left behind a layer of fresh dark soil, more precious to the farmers than fine gold. Then the fields were ploughed and planted, and by spring the crops of grain and flax were ripe for harvesting.

PLOUGHING
AND PLANTING
*From a wall
painting in a
tomb at Thebes*

The farmers could be sure of sunshine for the growing crops. They knew the sun-god Re would cross the sky each day. But the amount of the river's rising was unpredictable, and the flood could only be put to use by hard and constant work. They learned to store the water and lead it through canals to irrigate

19

the fields. Yet all their efforts were worthless if the waters failed to rise. A low Nile meant a lean year of poor harvest, or no harvest at all. Too great a flood would sweep away the mud-built towns and villages of the valley. The people would pray to Hapi, the god of the flood, to grant them a good year.

Although the flood was the concern of everyone, from the king to the humblest farmer, no one knew where the river came from or why the waters rose. Some said the flood came gushing from caves above Aswan, the river town that marked the southern boundary of the land. The Egyptians explored the Nile far above Aswan. They knew the rocky cataracts of the river in the country of Nubia, where they went to trade for ivory and to mine gold, but not even the boldest travelers had found the

20

sources of the Nile. They knew nothing of the tropical rains and melting mountain snows in the heart of Africa that swelled the river in the spring.

The White Nile, the river's longest branch, is fed by the lakes of Uganda. Today, if we sail along its upper reaches, just below Murchison Falls, we can see myriads of wildfowl and scores of crocodiles and hippopotamuses among the green papyrus, just as the Egyptians saw them in their own land long ago.

The Blue Nile rises in the north of Ethiopia near Lake Tana, where fishermen still glide between the wooded islands in slender papyrus boats. Below the lake the river changes from a broad slow stream to a raging torrent as it plunges with a roar of thunder over the escarpment of the Tississat Falls. It makes a huge bend through the highlands of Ethiopia, carving a mighty canyon in the hills, and meets the White Nile at Khartoum in the Sudan.

The river's northward course through ancient Nubia to Aswan is drowned today beneath the lake behind the new High Dam. Egyptian forts and temples along the old riverbank have been submerged. The rocky cataracts that hindered navigation

21

SMALL FAIENCE
FIGURE OF
A ROARING
HIPPOPOTAMUS

SHIP TRAVELING
UPSTREAM
UNDER SAIL
*From a wall
painting in
the tomb of
Menna, Thebes*

have disappeared, and the wide waters reach out to distant desert shores, where pointed hills spring up like pyramids.

Below Aswan the Nile was the highway of ancient Egypt, leading to the delta and the sea. The people could depend on the north wind to drive their ships upstream, and downstream the sails were furled and rowers bent to the oars.

Cargo ships carried grain and merchandise or huge blocks of Aswan granite for building. There were gay pleasure boats of kings and noblemen, and sad funeral boats bearing stone coffins for burial. Even the gods of Egypt traveled by boat from one temple to another.

The river was the link between north and south, between the lush delta country of Lower Egypt and the desert of Upper

22

Egypt, where the river valley was a band of blue and green across the sun-scorched earth. Upper and Lower Egypt were so different that the people thought of them as the Two Lands. In prehistoric times they had two separate rulers, and only when the Two Lands were united could Egypt become a great nation.

Two of the ceremonial titles, or "great names," of every king of Egypt proclaimed him ruler of the Two Lands. He wore a crown that combined in its form the crowns of Upper and Lower Egypt, and the thrones of royal statues often bore a carving to show the land united under the king. Two figures of Hapi, the Nile god, faced each other, one holding a papyrus plant, the symbol of the North, and the other with the lotus of the South.

A king named Narmer is believed to be the one who first united the Two Lands. The long narrow country, shaped by the river, would always be difficult to hold together in unity, and from the beginning the king needed strength and power that were more than human. His people in North and South must not only give him their respect and loyalty; they must bow down and worship him.

And so it was, at the dawn of Egyptian history, that kings became gods.

UPPER EGYPT

LOWER EGYPT

DOUBLE CROWN
OF THE TWO LANDS

UNION OF THE
TWO LANDS
*Carving from
a statue of
Ramesses II,
Luxor Temple*

PALETTE OF
KING NARMER
(BACK)
I Dynasty

Kings, Gods, and Animals

King Narmer came from Upper Egypt and was a warrior king. He led his army storming down the river, conquered the people of the delta and left a record of his triumph, carved in stone.

We see him here victorious, wearing the crown of Upper Egypt. He grasps a kneeling prisoner, seized in battle, and two more prisoners lie beneath his feet. The clump of papyrus, shown with the head of a man, is a symbol of the captured marshland of Lower Egypt, the country of papyrus. The falcon that holds the marshes captive for the king is the bird of Horus, the sky-god, and reminds all men that Narmer is more than a human conqueror. He is Horus himself, the god come to earth.

The god-king is a giant beside the other figures, and when he swings his mace to smash the prisoner's skull, he has none of the wild movement of a human warrior. He stands in majestic stillness.

This slab of dark slate, carved on both sides with a record of King Narmer's victories, is in the shape of a palette for grinding green eye paint, a valuable cosmetic and medicine.

25

IVORY STATUETTE
OF A KING
I Dynasty

PALETTE OF
KING NARMER
(FRONT)
I Dynasty

Large and elaborate as it is, the palette may have been used by
the king on ceremonial occasions. In the front of it there is a
round hollow to hold the powdered paint, framed by the twin-
ing necks of two fantastic animals. Above them the king appears again, marching behind his standard-bearers to see the

26

rows of slaughtered prisoners. The scene at the bottom shows him destroying an enemy city. The king is represented by a bull and the city by a curved wall with jutting buttresses.

This use of pictures, in a kind of symbolic shorthand, developed into Egyptian hieroglyphic writing. "Hieroglyph" means "sacred carving," and was the name given to Egyptian writing by the Greeks, when they saw the inscriptions carved on the walls of temples in the Nile valley. The Egyptians themselves called their writing *medew neter,* "speech of the gods," and they always looked upon it as a holy thing. Scribes were the only people who could read and write with skill, and they were held in great honor.

In the simple picture-writing that developed in Egypt at the end of the prehistoric period, the word for each object, such as a bee, a bull, or a man, was represented by a single drawing, but by the time of King Narmer there were also symbols to stand for separate sounds. At the top of the palette the king's name, *narmer,* is formed by two signs in a square frame. Vowels were not written, but there was an alphabet of twenty-four consonants. Other signs represented groups of two and three consonants combined, and simple pictures of objects were also used to make doubly clear the meaning of the words.

One way of writing the word *mer,* meaning pyramid, was to use the sign for *mr,* add the separate consonants *m* and *r* and put a picture of a pyramid beside them.

Such writing was complicated to learn but beautiful to look at, and to the Egyptians it was a form of art. Inscriptions could

27

HIEROGLYPHIC
INSCRIPTION
(*See page 51*)

be appreciated as much for their good design as for their meaning, and signs in the forms of living creatures were carved and painted with particular care and skill.

Egyptian artists, from prehistoric times, had a deep feeling for the birds and beasts and insects that shared their world. We see this in the carving of a stone memorial to King Uadji, a successor of Narmer. A graceful snake, representing the sound *dj,* stands for the king's name, and above it is the falcon of Horus. The sculptor has given the bird all the features of a falcon—the large eye and hooked beak, long wings and strong talons; but this is more than a fine rendering of a bird. It is a sacred bird, the symbol of a god, and it possesses a godlike dignity.

Almost every common animal in Egypt was associated with a god. Even the humble scarab beetle, rolling a ball of dung along the ground, became a symbol of the mighty sun-god who pushed the sun across the sky.

The vulture, soaring over the valley on motionless wings, was the bird of Nekhbet, the goddess who protected Upper Egypt. Wadjet, who guarded Lower Egypt, was the cobra-goddess, and her hooded snake adorned the crowns of Egypt's kings. The

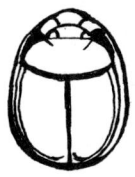

SEAL IN THE
SHAPE OF A
SCARAB

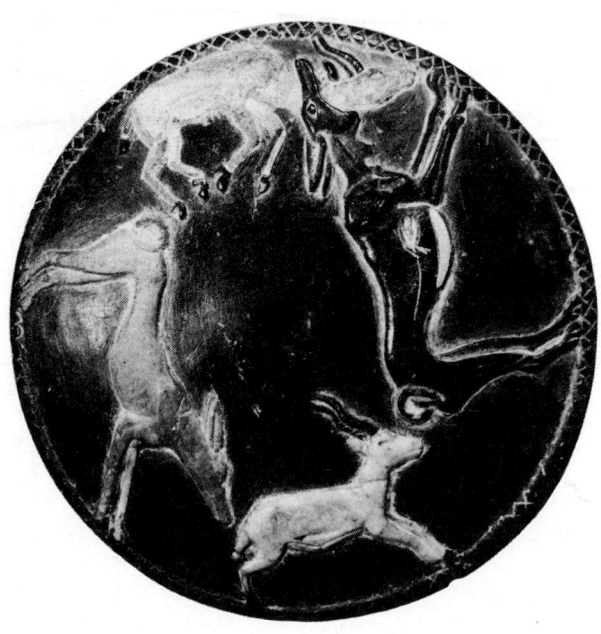

HOUNDS HUNTING
GAZELLES
(BLACK STEATITE DISK
INLAID WITH ALABASTER)
I Dynasty

FUNERARY STELE
OF KING UADJI
I Dynasty

THE GOD THOTH

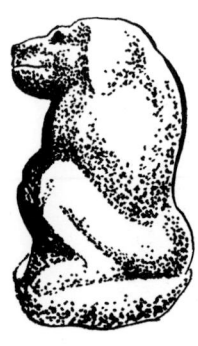

marshland ibis and the wise baboon were sacred to Thoth, the god of scribes; and Ptah, the creator-god and patron of craftsmen, might appear in the form of a bull. The gentle cow belonged to Hathor, goddess of the sky, whose head is shown with cow's horns at the top of King Narmer's palette.

There was a bewildering number of gods. Some of them were great and powerful, served in their temples by large companies of priests. Others were local gods, belonging to certain towns or worshiped by people in their homes. Often the gods were pictured as animals, or as men and women with animal heads. Their forms, and their names, might change, or several gods could merge together into one. When the sky-god Horus, with the king as his image on earth, merged with the sun-god Re, the people believed their king to be the son of Re. He was then an even more powerful god than before.

Opposite
IBIS IN PAPYRUS MARSH
*Detail of a relief
carving in a royal
tomb, V Dynasty*

SMALL SCHIST STATUE
OF KING KHASEKHEM
ENTHRONED
II Dynasty

Thirty dynasties of kings ruled over ancient Egypt through
its long history, from King Narmer in 3100 B.C. to the conquest of the land by Alexander the Great three centuries before
the birth of Christ. Not all the kings were strong, and there

were desperate times of civil war and foreign invasion, but as long as the Two Lands were united and the king proudly enthroned, he was the center of the nation's life. Then not even the richest nobleman could rival him in power. It was the king who built temples for the gods and elaborate tombs for himself and his family, and he alone commanded the labor of hundreds of workmen and the skill of the finest artists in the land.

When the slate palette was carved for King Narmer, the Egyptians' experience of art was small. With no long traditions of great architecture, sculpture, and painting to fall back on, they were launching out into the unknown. Artists leaped forward in an explosion of new ideas, inventing new forms and setting patterns that were to be followed for centuries to come.

The works of art we shall see in this book will lead us through fifteen hundred years, the years of Egypt's greatest splendor. Our story starts in the reign of King Zoser at the beginning of the Third Dynasty, when the Pyramids of Giza were still undreamed of. The stage was set for new ventures in art. The land of the Nile valley was rich and prosperous, sheltered from attack by the barriers of the desert. Artists were ready to work at the king's command, the materials were at hand, and all that was needed was a man of genius to lead the way.

STONE FIGURE
OF A FROG
Predynastic Period

II The Age of the Pyramid Builders

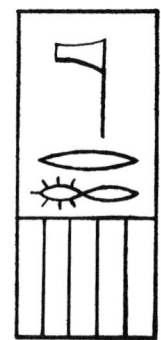

"Staircase to Heaven"

Imhotep, King Zoser's architect, was a man of genius and daring. His masterpiece, the Step Pyramid, still stands today, high on a desert ridge above the river valley and the ruined site of Memphis, the first capital of the Two Lands.

When King Zoser's body was carried there for burial, the Step Pyramid gleamed white in its facing of fine limestone, and along the ridge in front of it stretched a limestone wall with a lofty gateway. The passing of more than four thousand years has left the pyramid battered, rough, and brown, but it still towers over all the other tombs of Sakkara, the ancient city of the dead.

No king of Egpyt, before or since, had such a tomb as this. The kings before Zoser were buried in low, flat-topped buildings of mud-brick, which have become known as *mastabas,* from the Arabic word for "bench." Imhotep was the first to think of building a square *mastaba* of stone instead of brick. Then he enlarged his original plan until he had built five *mastabas* on top of the first one and created a step pyramid, the king's "Staircase to Heaven."

Imhotep did more than invent the form of the step pyramid and make it the first great stone building in the world. He surrounded it with other stone buildings in a vast courtyard.

MASTABA
TOMB

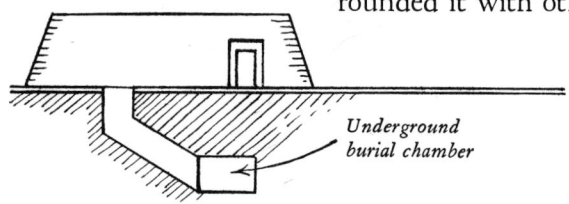

Underground burial chamber

34

STEP PYRAMID
OF SAKKARA
III Dynasty

Today, the walls of the court and some of the buildings have
been reconstructed after lying in ruins for centuries under the
drifting sand. We can approach the pyramid through the tall

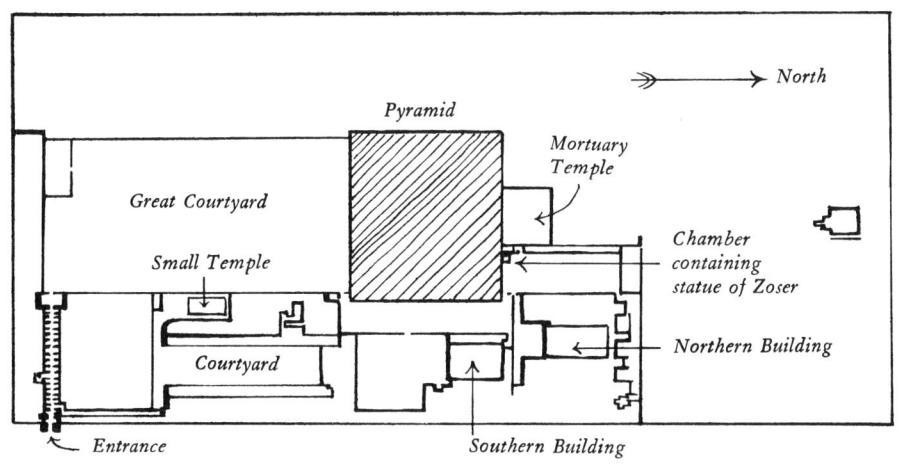

PLAN OF STEP
PYRAMID
AND COURTYARD

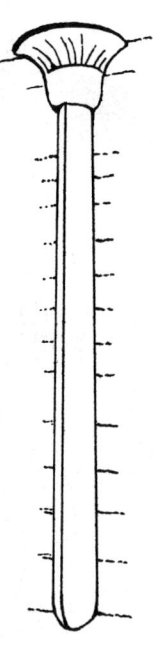

PAPYRUS-STEM
COLUMN

gateway, as in the time of King Zoser, and pass along a corridor within, between slender fluted columns. The courtyard, dominated by the mass of the pyramid, lies shimmering in the sun, and broken walls and pillars rise from the hot sand.

To the east are the ruins of two rows of small chapels with a long narrow space between them. Beyond the chapels are two buildings to represent the Two Lands, united under King Zoser's rule. The passage to the king's underground burial chamber goes down from the ruins of a temple, built against the pyramid's northern wall, and beside the temple we find a mysterious little room with roof and walls intact and two round holes for windows.

Dwarfed by the pyramid, the other buildings have an almost fragile look. White limestone columns are shaped like bundles of papyrus, or like the fluted stems of plants. Capitals of columns are carved in the form of papyrus heads, and stone ceilings are ribbed like roofs of rounded palm-tree logs. Perhaps Imhotep was copying in stone the wooden and mud-brick buildings of the king's palace. The king's tomb was also thought of as a palace, but it must be built to last forever.

When King Zoser's body was laid in the burial chamber, all who mourned for him believed that his immortal spirit, called the *ka*, was triumphantly alive. The *ka* would not only live on in the coffin with the king's body but could also move about the tomb, or mount the steps of the pyramid to join the sun-god on his daily journey across the sky.

The buildings in the courtyard were for the benefit of the king's spirit. The *ka* might even go through the ancient royal ceremony of the jubilee by running up and down the course between the two rows of chapels. In the king's lifetime this ceremony was performed after he had reigned for thirty years, and it was supposed to renew his youth and strength.

36

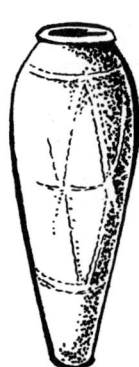

STONE VASE
From the Step Pyramid

The *ka* also needed to eat and drink, and daily food offerings were brought to the tomb by priests. To make sure of never-failing food supplies the rock-cut chambers beneath the pyramid were packed with hundreds of stone vases, which could be magically filled with food and wine by the recitation of spells. When the chambers were explored in modern times, many of the stone vases were still in place, undisturbed by the robbers who looted the tomb centuries ago and destroyed the bodies of King Zoser and his family.

Although the king's spirit was thought to dwell in his dead body, the destruction of the body did not leave the spirit without a home. In the little room beside the temple there was a substitute for the body. If we peer through the eyeholes in the wall, we see the gaunt craggy face of a life-size statue of the king.

37

ZOSER PERFORMING
A RELIGIOUS CEREMONY
*From a relief carving
under the Step Pyramid*

This statue is a copy of the one that was placed here at King Zoser's death and is now in the Egyptian Museum in Cairo. Damaged though it is, the statue can still give us the feeling of being in the presence of the king. The eyes, now gone, were probably inlaid with rock crystal in lifelike colors, and whoever cut them out in ancient times may have thought he was "killing" the statue. For this figure was not carved as a memorial of the king's past life. It was intended to be a *living image,* to insure that he would live forever in the future. By magic it could take the place of the king's body and give his spirit an eternal dwelling.

No one knows who carved the statue. The names of Egyptian sculptors, even the greatest of them, were not considered worth recording. The sculptor was simply a capable craftsman, the "wielder of the chisel."

Perhaps this figure of King Zoser, the oldest life-size statue to be found in Egypt, was carved by Imhotep himself. Besides being the king's architect and Overseer of Works for Upper and Lower Egypt, Imhotep was Chief Sculptor and Chief Carpenter. He was also famous as a High Priest, a scribe of great skill, a doctor of medicine, an astronomer, and a magician; and long after his death he was worshiped in Egypt as a god.

Imhotep was remembered with awe when the deeds of King Zoser were forgotten. Yet the king's name will live as long as his statue and his pyramid endure—two masterpieces that pointed the way to the wonderful works of the years to come.

39

The Pyramid Builders

The Step Pyramid had stood for a hundred years when King Khufu commanded the building of his pyramid at Giza, a tomb to surpass all others in size and magnificence.

The first tomb in the shape of a true, straight-sided pyramid was built by Khufu's father, King Sneferu. His pyramid stands in the desert at Dahshur, a few miles south of Sakkara, mighty in size but little known compared with his son's world-famous tomb, the Great Pyramid at Giza.

Herodotus, the historian of ancient Greece, was one of the first foreign visitors to see and to write about the Great Pyramid. He was in Egypt in the fifth century B.C., when the pyramid

Above
PYRAMID
OF KHUFU, GIZA

40

HEAD OF A KING
III–IV Dynasty

was more than two thousand years old. The priests who served as guides at Giza were full of lurid stories for the tourist, as guides often are. They told Herodotus that it took ten years to build the stone causeway leading to the pyramid and twenty to build the pyramid itself, with the constant labor of a hundred thousand men. They painted a grim picture of Khufu as an oppressor who earned the hatred of his people by enslaving thousands of them to build his colossal tomb.

The work must have taken many years and thousands of men, but far from being hated, Khufu was revered and worshiped, as his father had been before him. The welfare of the god-king, in this life and in the life to come, was the concern of the whole

41

country. In theory, at least, it was an honor to work on the king's "Castle of Eternity," even for those who labored at quarrying and hauling stone.

Probably most of the work was done in summers, when the Nile was in flood and the farmers were idle. The mighty stone blocks for the core of the pyramid, all weighing more than two tons, were quarried close to the building site. The fine limestone for the casing was cut in quarries across the river, and in flood-time it could be ferried over by boat almost as far as the pyramid. Then there was the endless task of dragging the stones on sledges up an earthen ramp to their places on the building. The ramp must have been made higher and higher as the pyramid rose, until at last the pointed capstone could be fitted on the top. Then, starting from the peak, the whole outer surface was smoothed and trimmed by skilled stonecutters, and the ramp stripped away as work progressed downward.

When the pyramid emerged, clean and polished and shining in the sun, the whole land must have rejoiced. The king had a tomb worthy of his greatness, and hidden in the heart of the pyramid his body would be safe forever.

The original entrance in the northern side, leading to the tomb chamber, was probably sealed and covered by casing stones after the king's burial. Today, almost all the casing is gone from the pyramid, and to enter we must clamber up between the huge blocks of the core. The narrow tunnel to the king's tomb chamber slopes steadily upward, then bursts into the Grand Gallery, with walls of polished limestone twenty-eight feet high. Awesome in its height and austere beauty, the gallery rises in a long incline, leading us deeper and deeper into the heart of the pyramid.

The tomb chamber is at the top, built of blocks of Aswan

granite fitted so perfectly together that not even a knife blade would slip between them. Nothing is left in the chamber but the granite sarcophagus, without its lid, that once held the king's body. Even this place was not safe from tomb robbers.

It is hard to picture the bare, echoing room as it must have been at the time of King Khufu's burial, piled high with offerings of food and flowers, with jewelry, vases, golden statues and furniture, and all that the king would need in the life to come.

The daily food offerings for his immortal *ka* were presented by the priests in the temple on the pyramid's eastern side. The long stone causeway that Herodotus saw linked this temple to another on the edge of the river valley. Each of the three Pyramids of Giza had two temples attached to it. Little can be seen of these buildings today, except for the valley temple of the second pyramid, the pyramid of Khafre, Khufu's son.

SECTION OF
PYRAMID
OF KHUFU

King's Chamber

Grand Gallery

"Queen's Chamber"

Chamber originally intended for king's burial

Pyramid of Menkaure

Mortuary Temple

Causeway

Valley Temple

Pyramid of Khafre

Mortuary Temple

Causeway

Sphinx

Valley Temple

Western Cemetery (Tombs of Nobles)

Pyramid of Khufu

Mortuary Temple

Causeway

Eastern Cemetery (Royal Tombs)

North

PLAN OF PYRAMIDS, TEMPLES, AND TOMBS AT GIZA

THE GREAT
SPHINX, GIZA

VALLEY TEMPLE
OF THE PYRAMID
OF KHAFRE

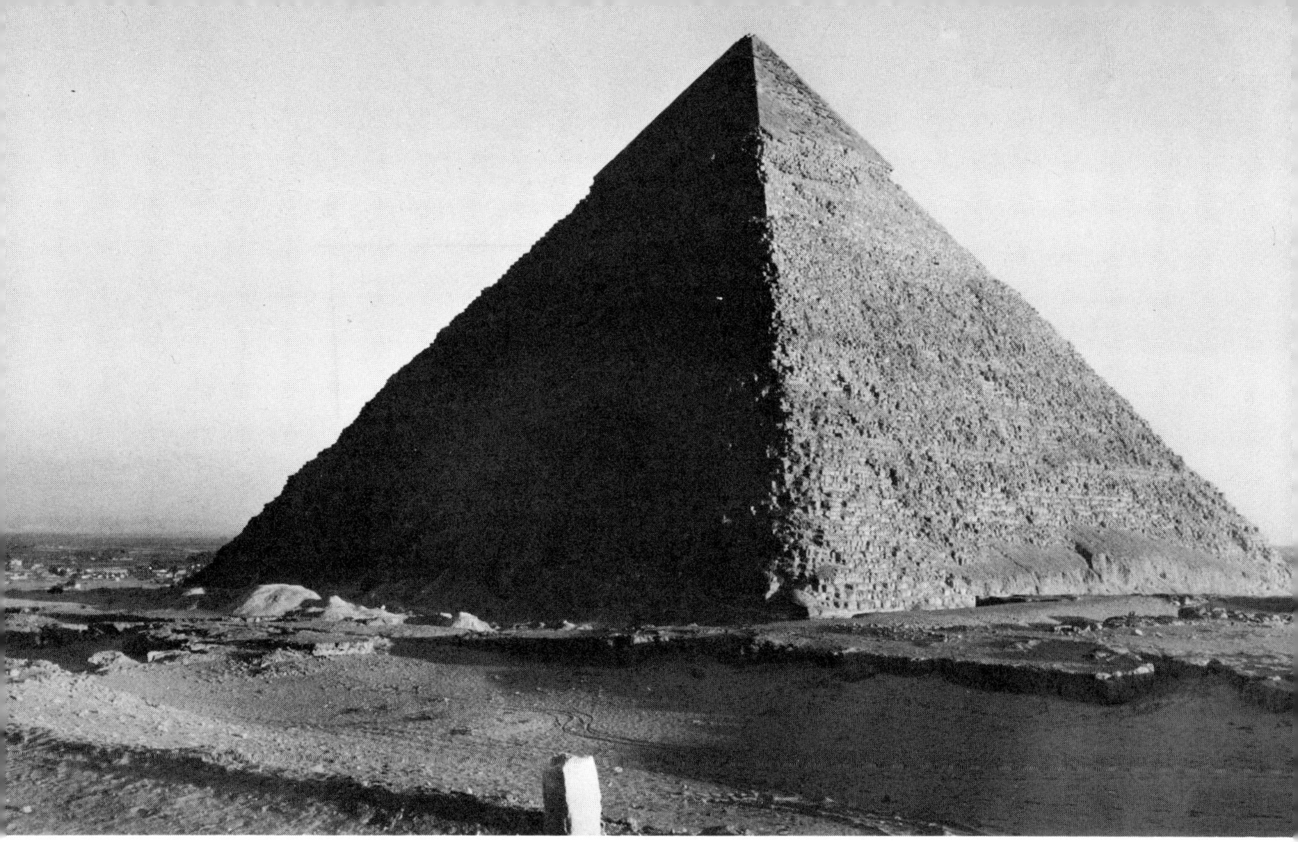

PYRAMID OF KHAFRE, GIZA

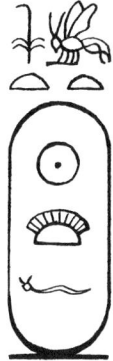

The face of Khafre is known the world over, for it is the face of the Sphinx. During the building of the second pyramid the Sphinx was carved from a mass of rock left standing in the stone quarry. The man-headed lion, looking eastward toward the sunrise, was a symbol of the sun-god and a guardian of the royal burial place.

Khafre's valley temple stands close by, as massive and majestic as the Sphinx. Here we find no imitation of wooden architecture, no delicate carving of papyrus and lotus flowers, but only the ponderous solidity of plain, undecorated stone. The temple was meant to be dark and mysterious. The sunlight that now blazes down between the square granite pillars was shut out. Light filtered into the temple hall through slits under the ceiling and gleamed on more than twenty statues of the king.

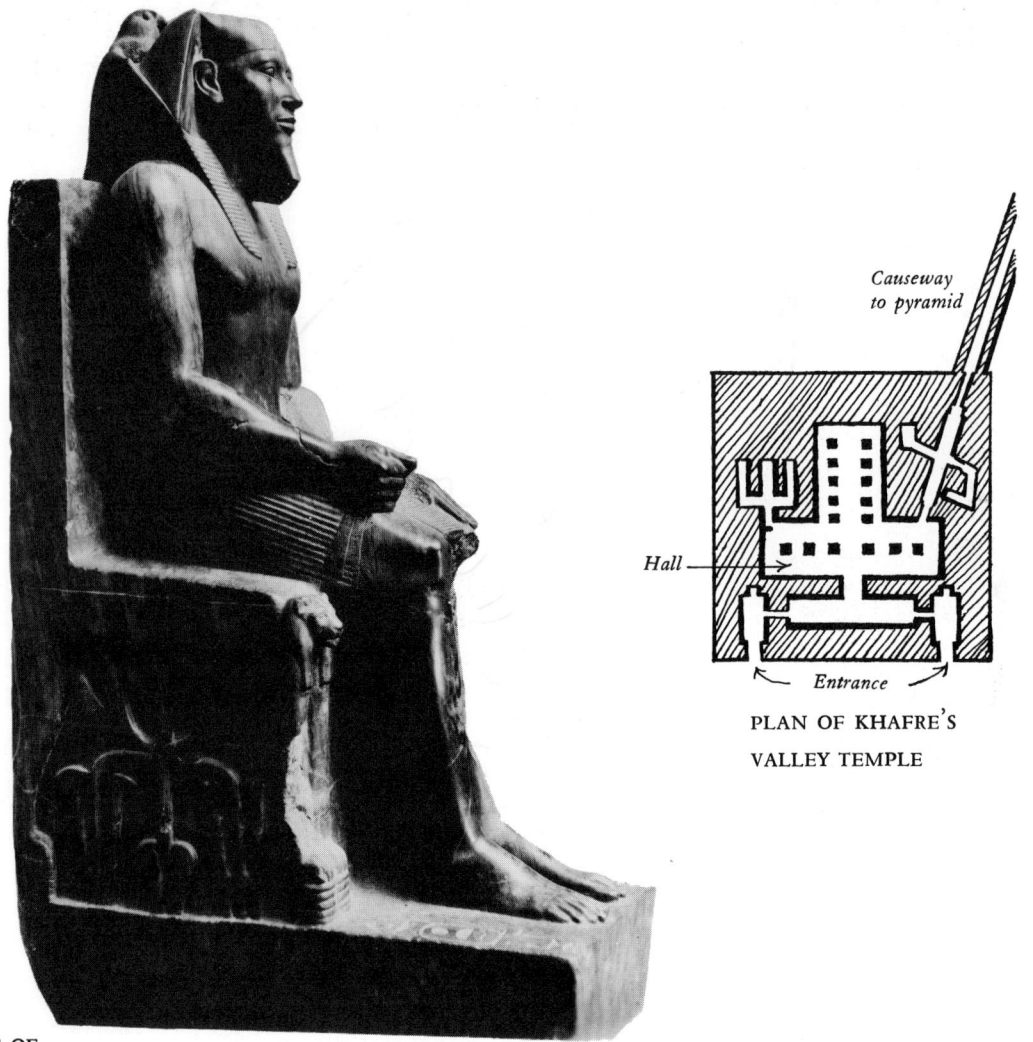

*Causeway
to pyramid*

Hall —

← *Entrance* →

PLAN OF KHAFRE'S
VALLEY TEMPLE

STATUE OF
KING KHAFRE
IV Dynasty

The valley temple was the starting point of the procession that carried Khafre's body up the causeway to the pyramid for burial. At the time of his funeral the priests went to each statue in the temple hall and performed the ceremony of "Opening the Mouth," so that the stone figures could become living dwelling places for the king's *ka*.

46

One of these living images of Khafre was found buried under the floor of his temple. The king sits enthroned, like the ancient figure of King Khasekhem (on page 31), and both statues show the sculptor's feeling for the hard, unbroken block of stone, the smooth simple form. Khafre wears a ceremonial beard and royal headdress, and behind his head, sheltering him with its wings, is the Horus falcon. Few statues express as forcefully as this one the serene power of the god-king.

HEAD OF
THE KHAFRE
STATUE

47

The third pyramid, smaller than the other two, was built by Khafre's son-in-law, Menkaure. According to Herodotus, he was a just and generous ruler, greatly loved by the people. We see him with his queen in a splendid sculpture that was found in the ruins of Menkaure's valley temple, along with many other statues of the king. The two figures, carved in dark gray slate, are regal in their proud, erect pose, but the queen's gesture with her arm about the king makes them seem human as well as god-like.

The upper part of the sculpture was smoothed and originally painted, but the lower part is still rough and the carved names of the king and queen are lacking. A statue was considered incomplete without its name. The carving of the name was an almost magic act and could make any statue—portrait or not—a true image of the person whose name was inscribed on it.

48

STATUE OF
KING MENKAURE
AND HIS QUEEN
IV Dynasty

Menkaure's tomb, like the other two pyramids, was looted by robbers, but one royal tomb at Giza was so well hidden that even robbers failed to find it. This was the deep, underground tomb of Khufu's mother, Queen Hetep-heres, near the Great Pyramid. The treasures discovered there can give us some idea of the wonderful works of art and craftsmanship that once filled the tombs of the kings.

49

REPRODUCTIONS OF THE
ARMCHAIR AND CARRYING
CHAIR FROM THE TOMB
OF QUEEN HETEP-HERES
IV Dynasty

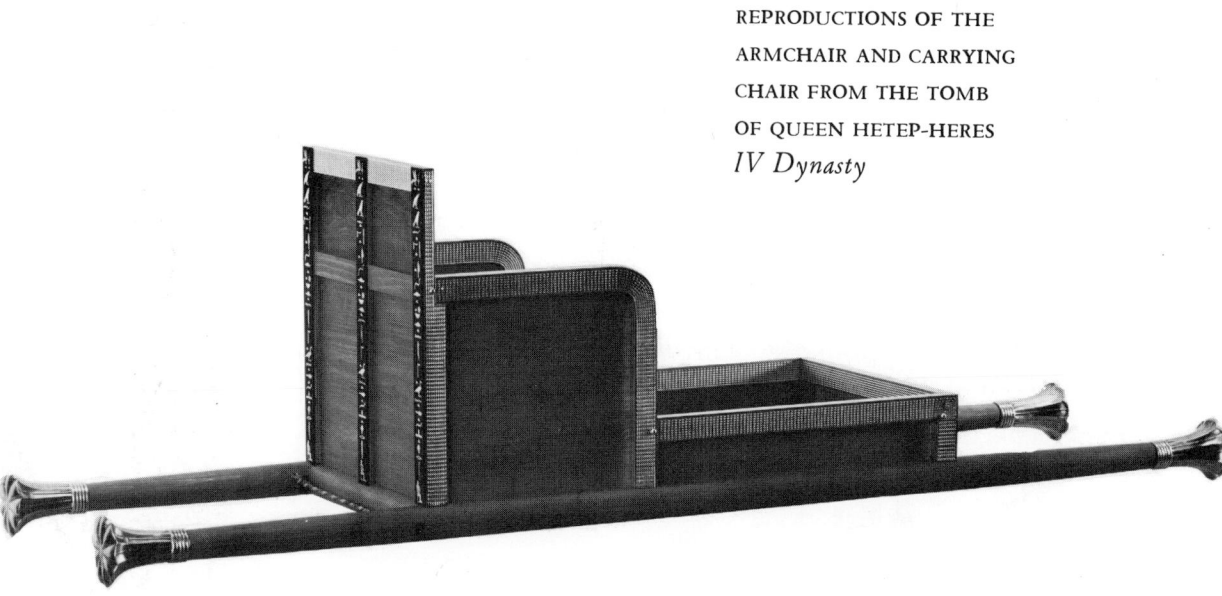

Crowded into a small chamber with the queen's stone coffin were alabaster vases and vessels of copper and gold; boxes for cosmetics and jewels; the queen's bed with its tall canopy; her armchair, plated with gold, and a carrying chair in which she could ride abroad, borne on the shoulders of her servants.

The carrying chair may have been a present to the queen from Khufu himself. The ebony strips on the back of it bear the queen's name and titles in golden hieroglyphs: "Mother of the King of Upper and Lower Egypt, Follower of Horus, Guide of the Ruler, Favorite One, she whose every word is done for her, the Daughter of the God's Body, Hetep-heres."

In the midst of the rich furnishings the queen's alabaster coffin was mysteriously empty. It is thought that she was originally buried somewhere else, probably near King Sneferu's pyramid at Dahshur, and that her tomb was robbed and her body destroyed. Afterward, everything the thieves had left was brought to Giza by priests or government officials and secretly buried in the royal cemetery, to lie undisturbed for four thousand years.

The royal cemetery was a whole town of flat-topped *mastaba* tombs that grew up east of the Great Pyramid during the reigns of Khufu and his successors. To the west were the *mastabas* of nobles and men who had served as the king's officials.

Several kings in the Fifth and Sixth dynasties built their pyramids at Sakkara, and here too we find the tombs of noblemen who had held high posts in government and at court. These people expected to enter everlasting life after death, but not to sail across the sky with the sun-god like their royal masters. Their hope was to enjoy forever all the good things of life that they had known in the valley of the Nile.

51

HIEROGLYPHIC INSCRIPTION *From the back of the carrying chair*

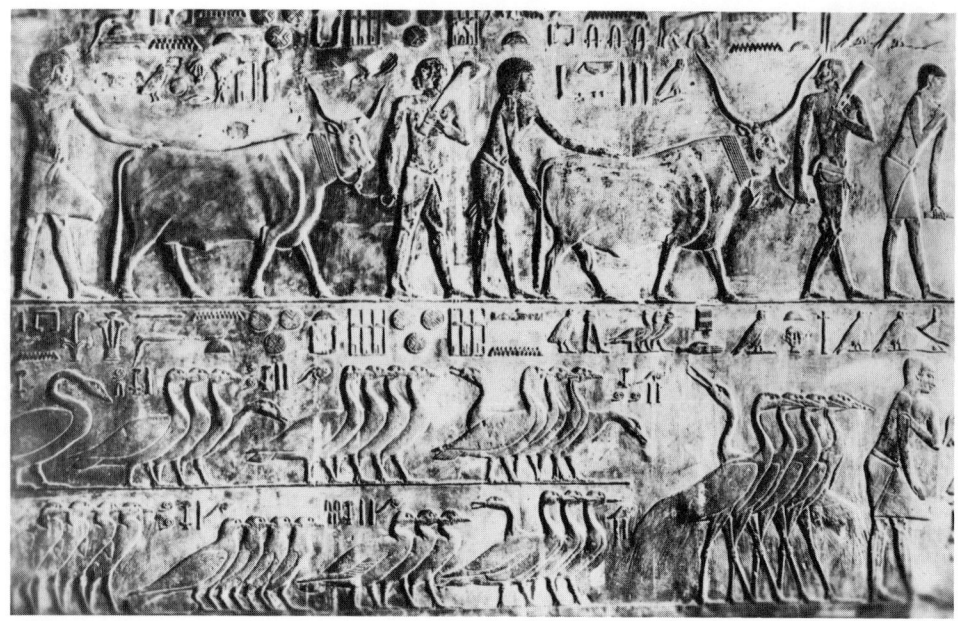

All the Good Things of Life

The tombs of the nobles at Sakkara had none of the austerity of the royal pyramids. The burial chambers were hidden deep below the ground, and the *mastabas* built over them like houses of many rooms. The tombs served as chapels where people could come with offerings, but, above all, they were cheerful homes for the spirits of the dead, filled with reminders of the bustle and hard work and gaiety of life along the river.

The owners of the tombs, from the highest government officials to the king's wigmaker and chief musician, were men of wealth. They owned large estates worked by scores of farmers, and they employed scribes to keep their records, and craftsmen to make furniture, pots and pans, and everything needful for comfortable living. All these people are pictured in the tombs,

Above FATTENED CATTLE, GEESE, AND CRANES
*From the tomb of Ptahhotep, Sakkara
V Dynasty*

52

carved in low relief and painted in red-brown, black and white, yellow, blue, and green. Hundreds of busy figures of people and animals are ranged in bands across the walls, like lines of writing in a book. Hieroglyphic inscriptions are fitted into the designs, as in the scene opposite, where the writing tells us how many thousands of fat geese and cranes there were. In the harvest scene above, the hieroglyphs show what the men are saying to each other as they reap the grain in time to the music of a flute.

"This is fine barley," says one man, and another shouts to a fellow worker, "Where have you got to, slow coach?"

In the tomb of a man named Ptahhotep the hieroglyphs even reveal the identity of the sculptor who carved the lively figures on the walls. At the foot of one wall there is a picture of a mock battle between men in papyrus-reed boats, and just out of reach of their thrashing poles we see the sculptor himself, peacefully seated in a boat enjoying a picnic lunch. His name is written above him: "The chief sculptor, Ankhenptah."

Above
HARVEST SCENE
Below
ROPING CATTLE
From the tomb
of Mereruka,
Sakkara
VI Dynasty

HUNTERS' RETURN
*From the tomb
of Ptahhotep,
Sakkara
V Dynasty*

Boys wrestling and marching and hunters returning from the
desert with captured animals are only a few of the figures carved
on this same wall by the sculptor Ankhenptah. The leading
hunters bring their greatest prizes, a lion and leopard, securely
caged and hauled along on sledges. Then come men with the

54

rolled-up skins of ibex and antelope and with hares and hedge-hogs in little cages. The last man has the hunting dogs, straining at the leash, and two ugly hyenas, also trained for hunting; and in the row below, men lead a long-horned oryx, an ibex, and small antelopes.

55

A tall figure of Ptahhotep, the owner of the tomb, stands solemnly waiting to receive the hunters' gifts. The desert animals and all the offerings pictured on the walls of the tomb—fattened cattle, geese and cranes, loaves of bread, and baskets of fruit—are nourishment for Ptahhotep's immortal spirit, meat and drink that his *ka* will enjoy forever.

In every properly equipped tomb stately processions of carved offering-bearers moved across the walls and converged at the false door, a painted niche in the wall above the underground burial chamber. Through this blind doorway the *ka* was supposed to enter the *mastaba* from the coffin below and partake of the offerings; and when gifts of real food and drink were brought for the *ka,* they were laid on a low table before the false door.

Lavish sacrifices must have been made in the great *mastaba* of a high official named Mereruka. His tomb had thirty-one rooms, and in the floor of the spacious offering chamber we can still see a stone ring for tying animals to be slaughtered. Here the niche above the offering table is filled by a painted limestone statue of Mereruka, striding forth to receive the gifts.

OFFERING BEARERS
IN THE TOMB
OF MERERUKA

A tomb was not complete without a statue of its owner, however many figures of him might be carved on walls and pillars. Like the sculptures of kings the tomb statues of private people were intended to be living images for the spirits of the dead to dwell in. They could also be wonderful portraits.

STATUE AND
OFFERING TABLE
Tomb of Mereruka,
Sakkara
VI Dynasty

57

Men and Women
Great and Small

Bedjmes was a shipbuilder who lived during the Third Dynasty, perhaps in the reign of King Zoser. He was probably a wealthy and important person, and he had reason to be proud of his craft. The building of ships for trade and travel on the Nile and in the Mediterranean was vital to the prosperity of Egypt. This granite statue shows Bedjmes sitting enthroned like a king, holding his adze, the shipbuilder's tool, as proudly as a scepter.

Statues of husbands and wives also followed the patterns set by royal sculptures. Memy Sabu and his wife, standing side by side, may remind us of Menkaure and his queen (on page 49). They are carved of white limestone and were originally painted, like the squat, round-faced figures of Katep and his wife.

Above STATUE
OF BEDJMES THE
SHIPBUILDER
III Dynasty

58

SMALL LIMESTONE TOMB STATUES:
Above MEMY SABU AND HIS WIFE
VI Dynasty
Right KATEP AND HETEP-HERES
IV Dynasty

Statues of scribes followed no royal pattern. The scribe was generally shown in a lifelike pose, sitting cross-legged and ready to write. On his knees would be a scroll of papyrus, the Egyptian form of paper, which was made from the pith of papyrus stems and used in long rolls for all kinds of records and writings.

At a time when few people could read and write, the scribes, as men of learning, were universally respected. Through education a man could rise to the highest positions in the land. Scribes often started life as poor village boys, and although they might never become high priests or kings' viziers, they could expect to have a far more comfortable career than farmers, soldiers, or craftsmen. We have only to compare the portrait of the alert, well-nourished scribe with the poor bony potter (on page 62) to see that this was true!

60

LIMESTONE STATUETTE OF
A BREWER STRAINING BEER
From a tomb at Sakkara
V Dynasty

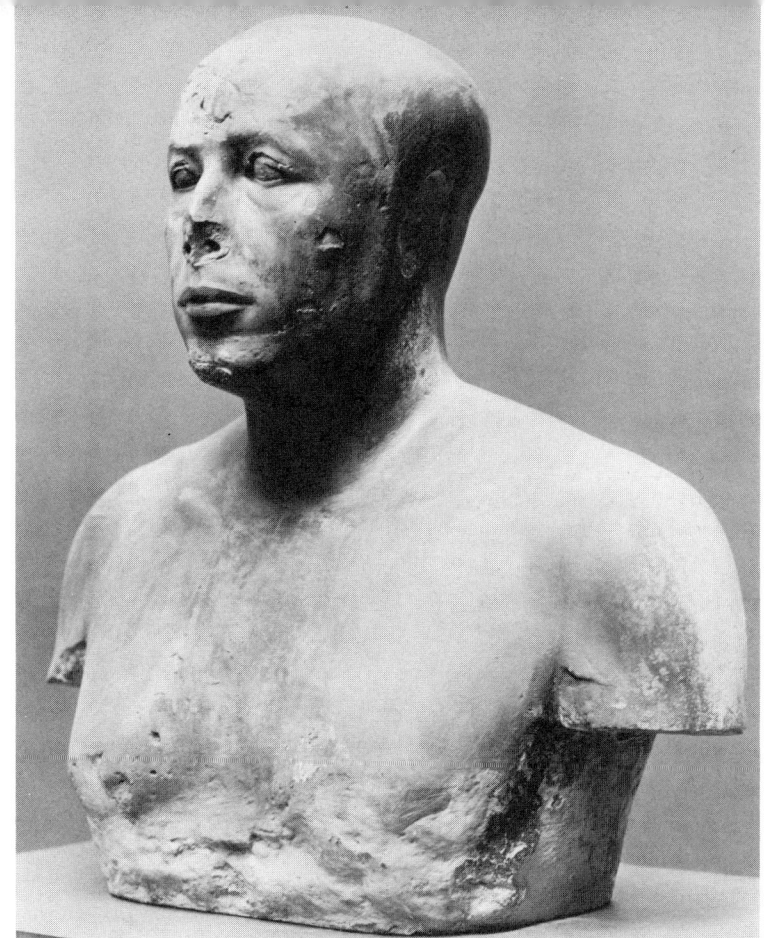

PORTRAIT BUST
OF THE NOBLEMAN
ANKH-HAF
*From his tomb
at Giza
IV Dynasty*

The little potter is one of the small servant-statues that were sometimes put in the tombs of their employers to work eternally at their appointed tasks. The potter's portrait must have been made from life, and his hunger and misery are shown with bitter humor.

In the strong face of Prince Ankh-haf we can see the suffering of a man in high office, working under the strain of responsibility. Ankh-haf, in this carved and painted portrait, seems as much a modern man as anyone we meet in the street. It is hard to believe that he lived four thousand years ago. He was the Overseer of Works under King Khafre, builder of the

61

SCRIBE AT WORK
*Relief carving from
a tomb at Giza
IV Dynasty*

second pyramid at Giza, and he saw the god-kings at the height of their power and glory. Could he or anyone have guessed at that time what disaster was to come?

Their mighty adventures in art were partly responsible for the downfall of the god-kings. Without a thought for the future of their country, they spent too lavishly, stripping the land of its wealth to build and furnish their tombs and temples. Meanwhile, the rich nobles were growing more powerful and living on great estates like private empires. The last king of the Sixth Dynasty reigned for over ninety years, until he was too old and feeble to hold the Two Lands together. Then war broke out among the nobles, and all the country's pride and confidence and strength crumbled away in strife between rival princes.

There was more than a century of turmoil before a strong leader arose to save Egypt from ruin. He mounted the throne as King Mentuhotep and earned the title of "He Who Unites the Two Lands." His long reign brought peace at last and began a new time of greatness, prosperity, and richness of art.

STATUETTE OF
A POTTER AT
HIS WHEEL
From a tomb at Giza
VI Dynasty

III *The Two Lands Reunited*

KING MENTUHOTEP
Relief carving from
his temple at Thebes
XI Dynasty

Sculpture and the New Spirit

Mentuhotep, who united the Two Lands, was a prince of Thebes in Upper Egypt, a little town that was to become famous throughout the ancient world.

Thebes and the temple of the Theban god, Amon, stood on the east bank of the Nile. On the west bank, where the barren hills of the desert overlooked the valley fields, Mentuhotep built a temple and a tomb. His temple was set on a terrace of masonry below a mighty rampart of limestone crags, and the tomb was dug deep into the rock at the cliff foot. The design of the temple, with its long colonnades, was new and original, but the small pyramid that rose abruptly in the center was an odd reminder of the splendid tombs of the past.

Mentuhotep's successors, kings of the Twelfth Dynasty,

64

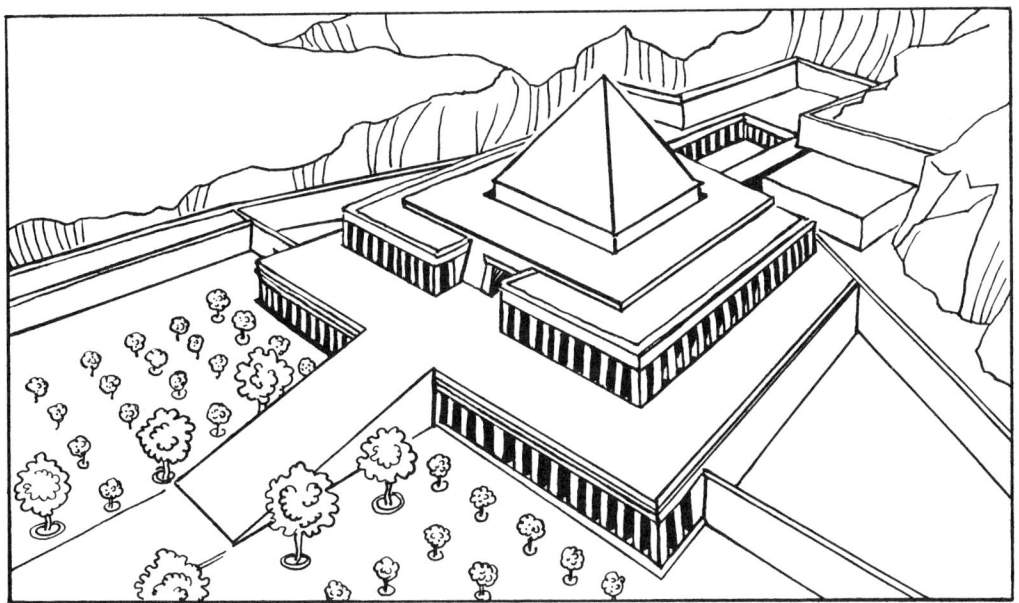

built themselves large pyramids in the old style, farther down the river, but none of their monuments could match the Pyramids of Giza. The time had passed when god-kings could command the building of tombs on such a scale. After the bitter years of trouble and strife there was a new spirit in the land.

Kings were still gods, but they were no longer so remote from their people. Mentuhotep and the kings who came after him felt deeply the burdens and responsibilities of kingship. They looked upon themselves as shepherds of their people, with a duty to care for them, to lead them, and to rule them with justice. Even poor farmers were no longer simply a source of labor for working the land or building pyramids, but were individual men whose rights must be respected.

RECONSTRUCTION
OF MENTUHOTEP'S
TEMPLE

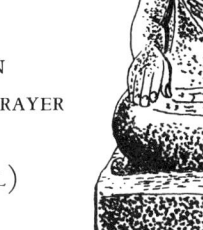

STATUETTE OF A MAN
(INSCRIBED WITH A PRAYER
TO THE GOD PTAH
FOR THE MAN'S SOUL)
XII Dynasty

KING SENWOSRET III
AS A SPHINX
XII Dynasty

Statues of kings reflected the new spirit of the time. King Senwosret III, one of the most powerful rulers of the Twelfth Dynasty, is shown in the form of a sphinx; but instead of a proud, godlike head we see the face of a man, sad-eyed and care-worn. He has none of the calm confidence expressed in the statue of King Khafre or in the Great Sphinx at Giza.

Change had also come to the Egyptians' beliefs about life after death. From the joyful, open-air worship of the sun-god in the blue sky, kings and their people turned to the worship of Osiris, god of the underworld. Osiris sat in judgment over the souls of the dead, and everlasting life was granted only to those who had done good deeds and avoided evil.

By now people were putting statues of themselves in temples, especially in the temple of Osiris at Abydos. The statues were humble figures, squatting or kneeling, and their simple blocklike shapes were inscribed with prayers. It was a comfort to a man to know that his statue was in a temple, offering endless prayers to the god on his behalf.

66

Above LIMESTONE
STATUETTE
XII Dynasty
Right STATUE OF THE
TREASURER SIHATHOR
XII Dynasty

**WOODEN
FIGURE OF
OFFERING-
BEARER**
*From the
tomb of
Meketre
XI Dynasty*

From the tomb of a nobleman named Meketre comes the painted wooden figure of a servant girl, which stands in gay contrast to the stone statues we have just seen. With a duck in one hand and a basket of food on her head, she is an offering-bearer, bringing nourishment for the spirit of Meketre. His rock-cut tomb at Thebes, not far from Mentuhotep's temple, was filled with wonderful wooden models of his servants going about their daily tasks. They rowed his boats on the river, caught fish for him, cooked his meals, made his bread, and looked after his cattle.

During the Eleventh Dynasty models like these were often placed in tombs, though few were as fine as those made for Meketre. The wooden figures must have been whittled by minor craftsmen in the workshops of sculptors, and most of them were more like children's toys than works of art.

Tombs at this time were more richly decorated with paintings than with sculpture. The painter covered the walls with his bold bright designs and adorned wooden coffins with writings and pictures. His work was meant to delight the spirits of the dead and also to help them on their terrible journey through the perils of the underworld.

WOODEN MODEL
OF A RIVER BOAT
*From the tomb of
Meketre
XI Dynasty*

The Art of the Painter

A line of fishermen, their red-brown bodies making a lively pattern, haul in a fine catch of fish from the river. Young dancing girls swing to the rhythm of hand-clapping, the clicking of bone clappers like castanets, and the music of flute and song.

These are two of the scenes painted in a tomb at Thebes belonging to Senet, the wife of a high official. A rock-cut passage leads to a single chamber with a painted statue of Senet and a shaft going down to her burial place below. All along the passage the pictures form a gallery of exciting designs. Wildfowl are trapped in a huge net and desert animals flee before the hunter, while busy servants in the household of Senet are drying beef, cooking ducks, and brewing beer from a mash of dates and dough.

The damaged picture of the dancers shows how the rough rock wall was covered with plaster of mud and straw to make a smooth surface for the paint. Sticks of soft wood, with one end

Above FISHERMEN
*Wall painting
from the tomb
of Senet, Thebes
XII Dynasty*

DANCERS AND MUSICIANS *Wall painting from the tomb of Senet, Thebes*
(THE SINGER IS THE FIGURE AT THE BOTTOM WITH ONE HAND HELD TO HER EAR)

PAINTING INSIDE THE COFFIN ON DJEHUTY-NEKHT
From his tomb at Deir el Bersheh
XII Dynasty

soaked in water and frayed into fibers, served the artist as brushes for applying the broad flat areas of color. He put in the fine outlines afterward with smaller brushes made from the frayed stems of rushes from the riverside.

Using these simple tools artists could produce paintings of miniature delicacy, as we can see in these pictures on the coffin of Djehuty-nekht. This man was one of the noblemen who governed the provinces of Egypt and ruled like little kings in their own cities. Djehuty-nekht lived at Hermopolis, downstream from Thebes, and not far away he made his tomb, hewn from the cliff above the river.

Thick planks of precious cedarwood were brought by ship from Lebanon to make his two big coffins, one fitting inside the other, and the artist who painted the outer coffin was as fine as any at the royal court. The body of Djehuty-nekht, when laid on its side in the coffin, would face this picture of the dead man with a lavish spread of food. The haunches, heads, and hoofs of animals, ducks alive and dead, loaves of bread, and jars of wine are painted in exquisite detail, brilliant against the reddish-brown of the wood. Behind the figure of Djehuty-nekht is the false door through which his *ka* was supposed to move in and out of the coffin.

The magic texts, thought necessary for the dead man's survival in the underworld, were written inside the coffin in line after line of tiny hieroglyphs, engraved and painted. In the days of the pyramid builders these writings could be inscribed only in the tombs of kings, but the royal texts were now also used by powerful nobles. *The Book of the Two Ways,* copied in Djehuty-nekht's inner coffin, even provided a map for the guidance of the dead man, as well as magic spells to help him overcome the dangers on the dark road to the kingdom of Osiris.

73

OFFERING-BEARERS
Detail from the
painted coffin

Khnumhotep, Governor of the Eastern Desert, was another wealthy nobleman. His tomb was cut in the cliffs of Beni Hasan, a short trip down the Nile from Hermopolis, and there we find this splendid picture of him trapping wildfowl in a lotus pond.

The artist has a keen eye for the wildlife of the river valley. The ducks and geese in the water and the shrikes and crested hoopoe in the little trees seem far more real than the stiff figures of Khnumhotep and his servant. The artist could paint birds as he pleased, but for the human figures he had to follow rigid rules that had been passed down from the beginnings of Egyptian history and art. The head of a man must be drawn in profile with the eye in front view. The shoulders must be seen from the front, the legs from the side.

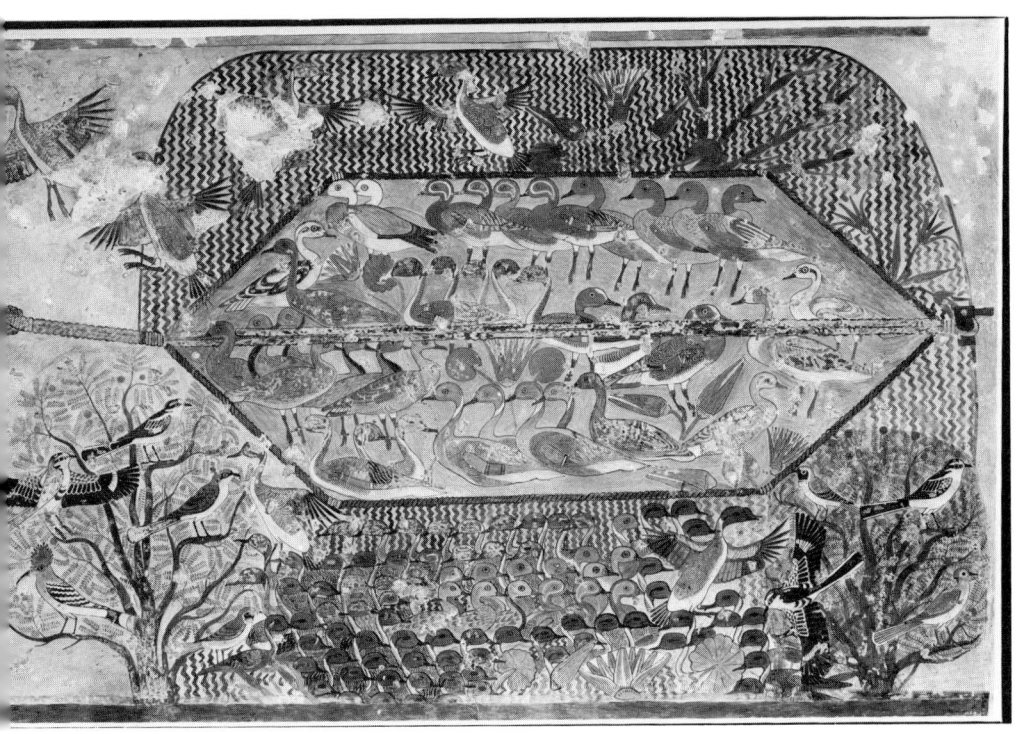

The designer of the ancient palette of King Narmer had followed these same rules of drawing. He also made the most important person in his picture much larger than anyone else, just as Khnumhotep has been painted here. Even the arrangement of rows of figures on the Narmer palette was a pattern followed in wall paintings and reliefs for hundreds of years.

The Egyptians hated change, and their ancient ways of drawing seemed to them to make pictures plain and easy to read. Painters and relief sculptors were trained to show the most typical and understandable view of everything, whether it was a man's eye or a pond full of ducks. An eye looked most like an eye when seen from the front, while a duckpond should be viewed from above in order to show the whole area of the water and all the birds that swam there.

FOWLING SCENE
Copy of wall painting in the tomb of Khnumhotep, Beni Hasan XII Dynasty

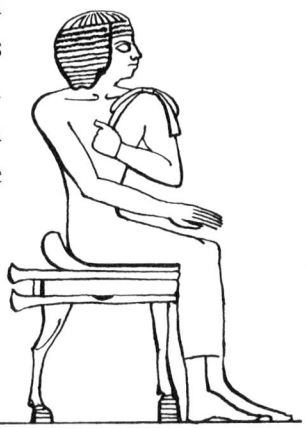

75

The rules for drawing people gave the chief figures in a picture a certain stillness and dignity, which makes Khnumhotep look more like a king enthroned than a man hauling on a rope. Less important people, such as these bearded nomads of the desert

DESERT NOMADS *Copy of a wall painting in the tomb of Khnumhotep, Beni Hasan XII Dynasty*

with animals as gifts for Khnumhotep, could be drawn more freely. Like the hunters we saw in the tomb of Ptahhotep, these men are shown with their shoulders in side view. Their gaily striped clothes and the cut of their beards and hair are carefully painted by the artist, who probably saw the caravan of nomads arriving at the mansion of Khnumhotep. The two men are part of a long procession of desert folk on the wall of the tomb, and among the goods they bring as tribute to the Governor of the Eastern Desert is the indispensable green eye paint.

Cosmetics and rare perfumes ranked with jewelry as essential for the proper adornment of well-dressed men and women. Khnumhotep himself probably had an elegant box, like the one above, for his alabaster jars of perfume and polished metal mirror. He almost certainly possessed some fine jewelry too, brilliant in color and exciting in design, for this was the golden age of the Egyptian jeweler's art.

77

WOODEN STATUETTE
OF A FOREIGN WOMAN
*From a tomb at
Beni Hasan
XII Dynasty*

CROWN OF PRINCESS SIT-HATHOR-YUNET *XII Dynasty*

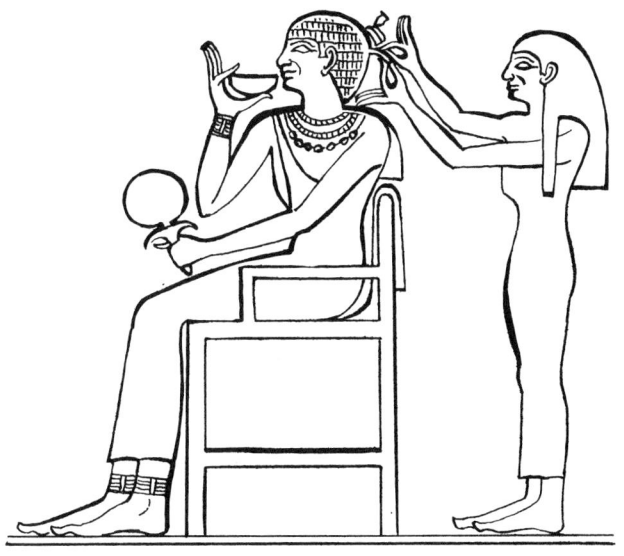

Jewels for Princesses

Sit-Hathor-yunet was the daughter of a king of the Twelfth Dynasty, Senwosret II, and her jewelry was worthy of a princess.

Here we see her golden crown with its long pendants of little gold tubes to fit over her hair. The circlet is inlaid with red carnelian and lapis lazuli in delicate flower designs. At the back rise two tall stylized plumes, and in the front is the sacred serpent of Wadjet, the cobra-goddess of Lower Egypt and the protector of kings.

The wonderful collection of jewelry that the princess must have worn while she lived was buried with her at her death. The tomb of Sit-Hathor-yunet, near her father's pyramid, was plundered many centuries ago, but her three ebony caskets of jewelry, sealed up in a secret hiding place in the wall, lay undiscovered until our own time.

TOILET OF
A QUEEN
*Carving from
the coffin of
Queen Kawit
XI Dynasty*

CARVED STONE
OINTMENT JAR
XII Dynasty

79

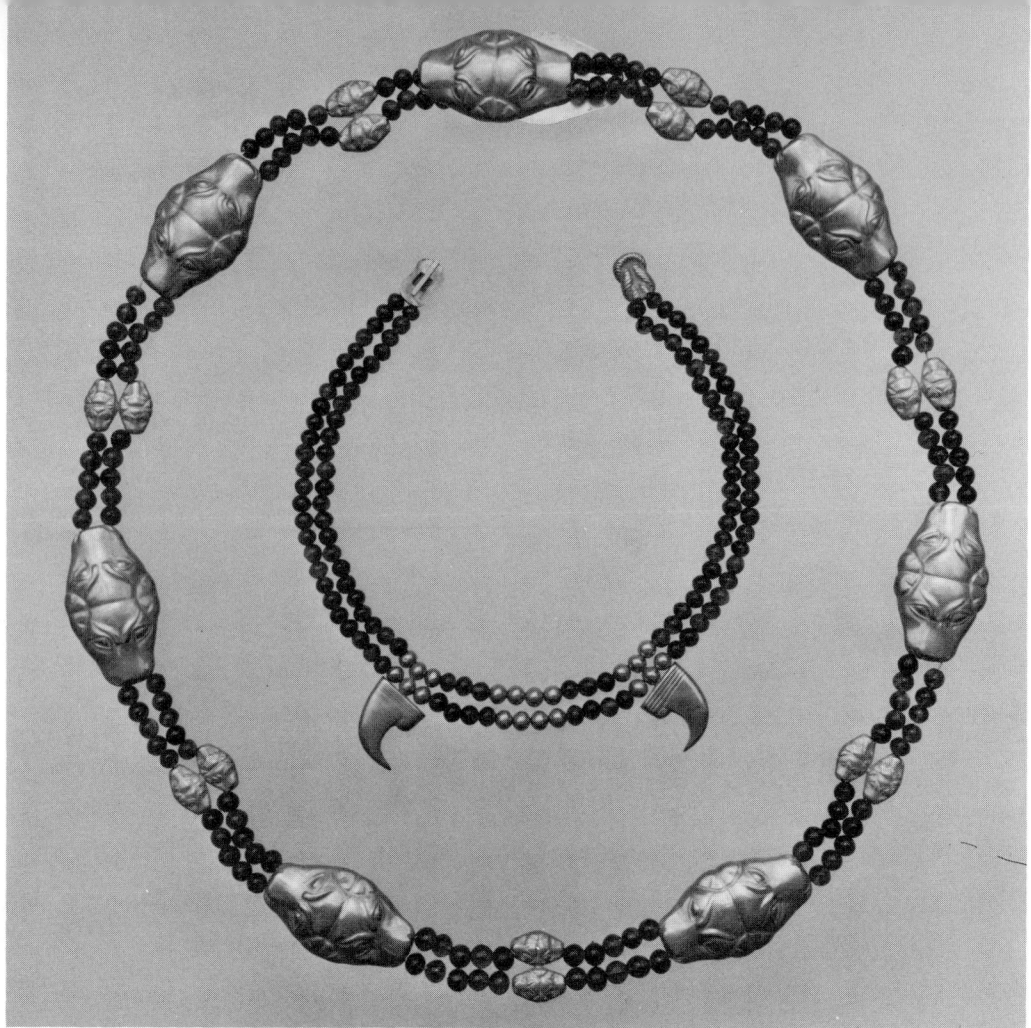

The girdle of beads was probably for informal wear in the private rooms of the palace, but it was as finely wrought as the ceremonial crown. The gold beads are in the shape of double leopard heads, and even the tiny ones are perfectly modeled and engraved. The gold and amethyst beads of the anklet were originally part of a necklace. Pendants to hang from necklaces were a favorite form of jewelry, and the greatest treasure of the princess was a magnificent pendant of gold, inlaid with lapis lazuli, carnelian, garnet, and blue-green turquoise.

80

INLAID GOLD PENDANT
OF PRINCESS SIT-HATHOR-YUNET
XII Dynasty

BACK OF THE
PENDANT
(ENGRAVED GOLD)

This pendant may have been a gift from her father, for the king's name appears in the oval cartouche at the top, between the two Horus falcons and the two cobras. From the bodies of the snakes hang two "ankh" signs, meaning life. The kneeling figure signifies "millions"; the sign for "hundred thousand" hangs from its right arm, and in both hands are palm branches, which stand for "years." The whole design can be read as a hieroglyphic inscription meaning "The sun-god gives many hundreds of thousands of years of life to Senwosret II."

When these words were worked in gold and jewels, it must have seemed as though no power on earth could shake the god-kings of Egypt and that their majesty was truly everlasting. Yet the end of the Twelfth Dynasty marked the beginning of another dark and stormy period in Egypt's story.

81

COLLAR OF BEADS
*From painting on the
coffin of Djehuty-nekht
XII Dynasty*

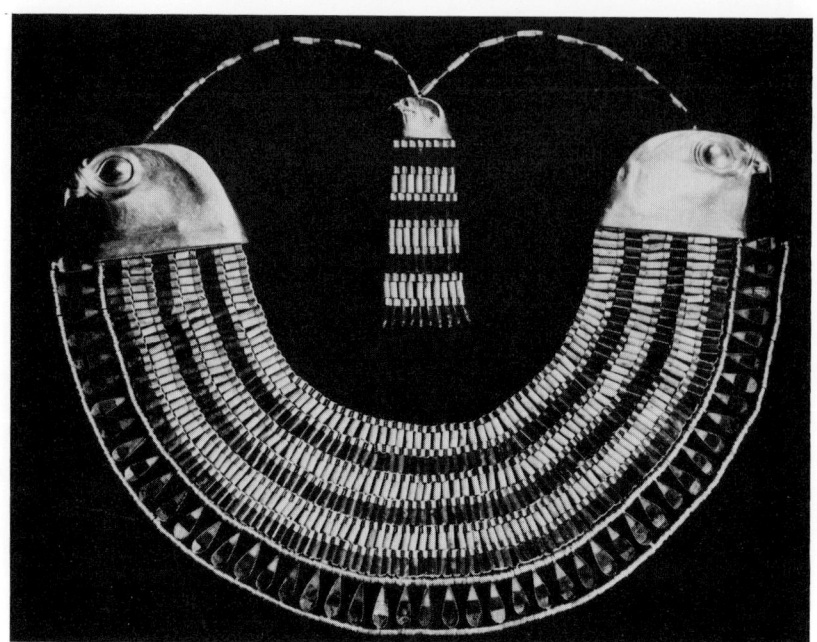

COLLAR OF BEADS
(GOLD, CARNELIAN,
AND FELSPAR WITH
GOLD HAWKS'-HEADS)
From the jewelry
of Princess
Neferwptah,
daughter of
King Amenemhat III
XII Dynasty

The Two Lands split apart, and the delta country was overrun by invaders from Asia—the terrible Hyksos, "Rulers of Foreign Lands." A tough, warlike people, they brought the first horses to Egypt and showed the Egyptians the deadly use of swift horse-drawn chariots in battle.

The Hyksos kings set up their own capital at Avaris in the delta and tried to bring the whole land under their rule, but they could never subdue the proud princes of Thebes. It was a Theban prince who rose to defy them and to strike the first blows for liberation; and after years of hard fighting the Hyksos were routed and sent fleeing eastward into Syria.

The Two Lands were united under the warrior kings of Thebes, and a new and magnificent age began—the Age of Empire.

IV Thebes and the Age of Empire

"Splendid Are the Splendors of Amon"

One of the most extraordinary rulers of the Age of Empire was Queen Hatshepsut. She first came to the throne as regent for her young stepson, Thutmose, then seized the full royal power and ruled in her own right. She declared herself to be the daughter of the great god Amon-Re of Thebes, divinely appointed to rule the land and to receive at her death a royal burial. Her tomb was to be on the western shore of the Nile at Thebes, and she built there a magnificent temple dedicated to her divine father and proudly called "Splendid Are the Splendors of Amon."

Many statues of the queen, clad in a king's regalia, were set up in her temple. This colossal granite figure shows her crowned with the White Crown of Upper Egypt and even wearing a man's short kilt and ceremonial beard as she kneels to present an offering of wine to Amon-Re.

Thebes was again the capital of the Two Lands, and the Theban god Amon, who had merged with the sun-god Re by the beginning of the Twelfth Dynasty, was the king of all the gods of Egypt. His temple at Karnak, in the town of Thebes, was the richest and most glorious in the land, enlarged and adorned and endowed with gifts by each successive king. The greatest of the yearly festivals at Thebes were in honor of Amon. In the joyful

85

GRANITE STATUE OF QUEEN HATSHEPSUT
From her mortuary temple at Deir el Bahri, Thebes, XVIII Dynasty

SPHINX OF
QUEEN HATSHEPSUT
*From her temple
at Deir el Bahri,
Thebes*
XVIII Dynasty

SISTRUM

Feast of the Valley the statue of the god was carried from the temple of Karnak in a richly decorated boat and taken across the Nile in a golden barge to visit the city of the dead and the tomb-temple of the reigning king.

When Amon's statue visited the temple of Queen Hatshepsut, the barge bearing the boat of the god would glide up a canal from the river's western bank to the edge of the desert. The priests would then take the god's boat on their shoulders and turn toward the temple along an avenue of stone sphinxes, each carved with the head of the queen. Dancers, singers, and musicians would accompany the procession, and all would move to the rhythmic jingle of the shaken sistrum and the chanting of sacred song. Offering-bearers would bring fruit and flowers and fattened cattle for sacrifice, and the people of Thebes would swarm across the river with gifts for the tombs of their relatives, so that the dead and living together might taste the joy of the feast.

86

The queen's temple could be seen from afar, set in the same awesome bay of the cliffs as that of King Mentuhotep, built many years before. The older building, with its ramp and terrace and colonnades, had inspired the new one, but the queen's architect, Senmut, had built no pyramid. The horizontal lines of the

TEMPLES OF QUEEN HATSHEPSUT (*Right*) AND KING MENTU- HOTEP (*Left*) *Deir el Bahri*

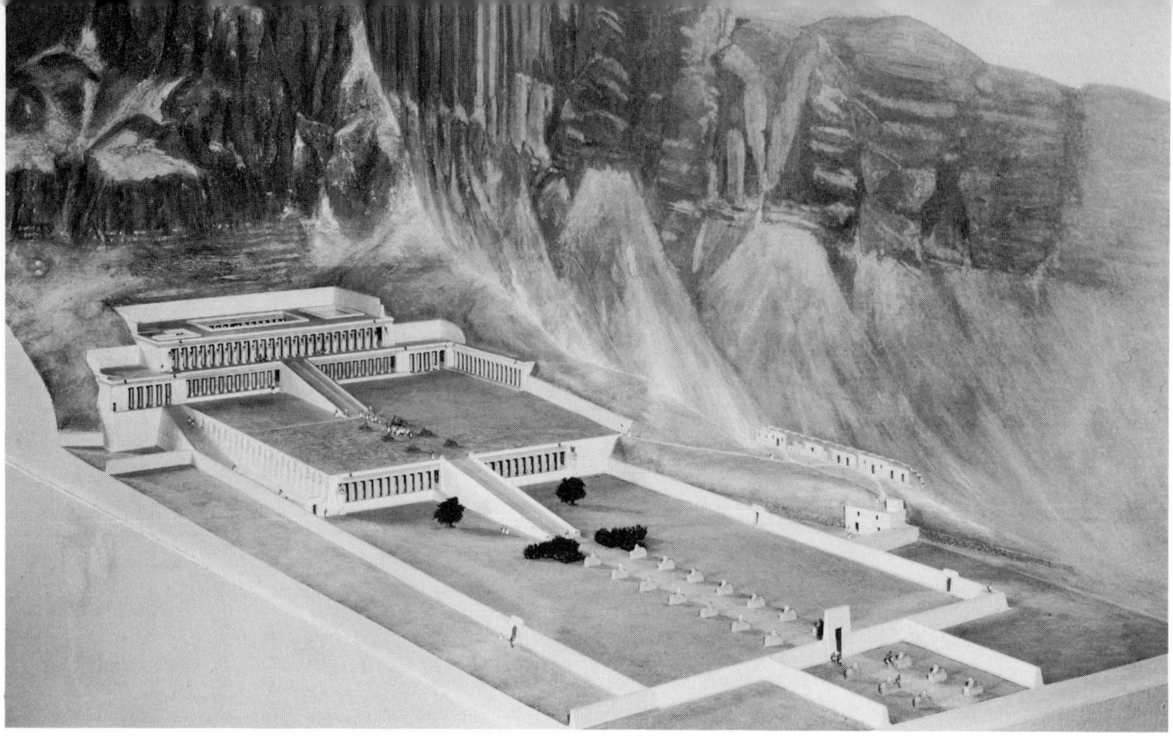

MODEL OF
THE TEMPLE OF
QUEEN HATSHEPSUT:
VIEW FROM
SOUTHEAST

queen's temple were in stark contrast to the towering cliffs. The decoration of carved and painted reliefs was hidden behind the colonnades, and the rows of columns in the sun-glare made a simple pattern of light and shade.

As the god and his retainers moved up the ramp to the first terrace, they saw before them a colonnade of fluted columns with the second ramp in the center and a chapel at each end. To the north was the Chapel of Anubis, the jackal-god who ruled the city of the dead, and to the south, reaching out toward the temple of Mentuhotep, was the Chapel of the gentle goddess Hathor.

In hidden corners of the Hathor Chapel the architect Senmut had dared to place his signatures—tiny figures of himself carved on the walls. As the queen's favorite minister, he was a man of power and held many offices, even serving as "Great Nurse," or tutor, to the queen's little daughter Nefrure.

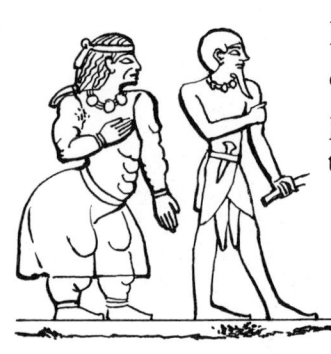

RULER OF PUNT
AND HIS WIFE
From reliefs in the temple of Hatshepsut

On the walls of the porch adjoining the Hathor Chapel the carved reliefs told the story of an expedition to Somaliland, called by the Egyptians the Land of Punt. Amon himself, the queen declared, had commanded her to send men to search out the way to Punt and "explore the roads to the terraces of myrrh." She thereupon ordered five ships to sail down the Red Sea, and the artist who recorded their achievements must surely have made his drawings on the spot.

When the Egyptians reached the East African coast, the people welcomed them, led by the ruler of Punt and his stout wife. Myrrh trees were plentiful in their country, and they

STATUE OF
SENMUT WITH THE
PRINCESS NEFRURE
XVIII Dynasty
(See page 67)

HOUSE ON STILTS IN
THE LAND OF PUNT
From reliefs in the
temple of Hatshepsut

89

gladly brought the strangers the precious gum of the trees, which was burned as incense in Egyptian temples and used in cosmetics and medicines and for embalming the bodies of the

RELIEF CARVINGS
OF THE EXPEDITION
TO PUNT:
PRODUCE OF
PUNT BROUGHT
TO THE EGYPTIANS

dead. Not only the gum but the living trees were loaded aboard the Egyptian ships, along with elephant tusks, live baboons, and bags of gold. The expedition and the finely carved reliefs that told its story were both alike a triumph for the queen.

Perhaps some of the myrrh of Punt was burned in her temple at the Feast of the Valley, when the sacred boat of Amon was carried up the second ramp and approached the sanctuary. The priests passed through the colonnade of the upper terrace, where each square pillar was faced with a figure of the queen in the guise of Osiris, god of the underworld. Then the people, watching from afar, saw them no more. The god had entered the Holy of Holies, cut deep into the rock of the mountain, and the people dispersed over the bare slopes below, carrying their gifts to the rock-cut tombs.

Today, the hillside south of the queen's temple, honeycombed with mysterious holes and heaped with the rubble of ancient and modern diggings, hides a whole world of beauty and delight. In the depths of the tombs there is color and warmth and humor, where the hands of long-dead artists have given eternal life to the people of Egypt and the empire.

91

HALL OF THE TOMB OF MENNA, THEBES *XVIII Dynasty*

Famous Men of Thebes

Entering the tomb-chapel of Menna at Thebes, we are plunged at once into the activity of the man's official life. Although the picture at the end of the entrance hall shows Menna and his wife worshiping Osiris and reminds us that this is a tomb, it is life, not death, that seems to fill these rock-cut rooms. As in the old *mastabas* at Sakkara, the burial chamber is hidden below the floor. The painted tomb-chapel is a place for offerings and a "house of eternity," where the spirit of the dead man can enjoy the delights and the labors of his years on earth.

Menna held an important post as "Scribe of the Fields of the Lord of the Two Lands," and in the large painting on the left he watches over the work of the harvest. The painter of the picture put in small touches of his own that make the scene come alive. Two girls, who followed the harvesters to glean the stray ears of grain, are fighting over their shares of the takings. Two men rest under a tree in the day's heat, with a waterskin hanging from a branch, and one of them plays the flute.

Shrine

Passage

Hall

Courtyard

93

PLAN OF A TYPICAL
ROCK-CUT TOMB-
CHAPEL AT THEBES

WALL PAINTING
IN THE TOMB
OF MENNA, THEBES
XVIII Dynasty

At the top of the picture a field of ripe barley is measured to calculate how much grain must be paid in taxes. At the bottom the reapers are at work, and the ears of barley are carried away to

be threshed. In the center workers are winnowing, tossing up the grain to separate the chaff, and finally eight scribes record the amount of the harvest.

A more important official than Menna was the vizier Rekhmire who served King Thutmose III, the stepson of Hatshepsut.

In his high office, second only to the king himself, Rekhmire received the tribute brought to Egypt by people from the distant lands of the empire. These tribute-bearers march in procession along the wall of the entrance hall of his tomb—bearded Syrians leading fine horses, a bear, and a surprisingly small elephant; slim-waisted Cretans bearing costly vases; and Nubians from Egypt's southern frontier with long-horned cattle and hunting dogs, and a beautiful giraffe that the artist must have drawn from life.

Like most of the tomb-chapels, that of Rekhmire shows us a whole army of craftsmen at their varied work. Sculptors and woodworkers, tanners of hides, and makers of bricks and rope are crowded together along one wall of the passage that leads from the entrance hall to the rear chamber of the tomb.

Here we see metalworkers burnishing vases and carpenters busy with bow-drill and saw, making chests and a funerary bed with carved lions' heads. Among the other workers is an energetic band of men who hoist up heavy jars of wine and bundles of papyrus stems, destined for the treasury of Amon's temple.

FEASTING SCENE
*Wall painting from
the tomb of Nebamun,
Thebes
XVIII Dynasty*

The pleasures of life, as well as its responsibilities, were not forgotten in the tomb-chapels. Although stout and dignified men like Rekhmire probably never went duckhunting in the marshes in flimsy papyrus boats, they still included this traditional scene among their tomb paintings (see page 19). Most of these great men, however, must have enjoyed feasts with their friends, such as we see in so many of the tombs. The old simple picture of the dead man seated before a table of food had become a dinner party on a grand scale, with rows of guests entertained by dancing girls, singers, and musicians. The painting opposite, giving us a glimpse of the luxurious life of the rich in the Age of Empire, is particularly interesting for the artist's break with convention. He shows a rare fullface view of two of the entertainers and even reveals the soles of their feet! The little dancers, too, have a new ease and rhythm of movement.

But the artists still enjoyed their greatest freedom when painting animals. In a hunting scene in the tomb of the steward Kenamun the animals have the grace and tension of living creatures. They are no longer arranged in rows across the picture. We find them set in a desert landscape of winding stony paths and sheltered hollows—an ostrich, a sleeping calf, a wild ass, and this noble ibex, attacked by a hound.

IBEX AND HOUND
Copy of a
wall painting
in the tomb of
Kenamun, Thebes
XVIII Dynasty

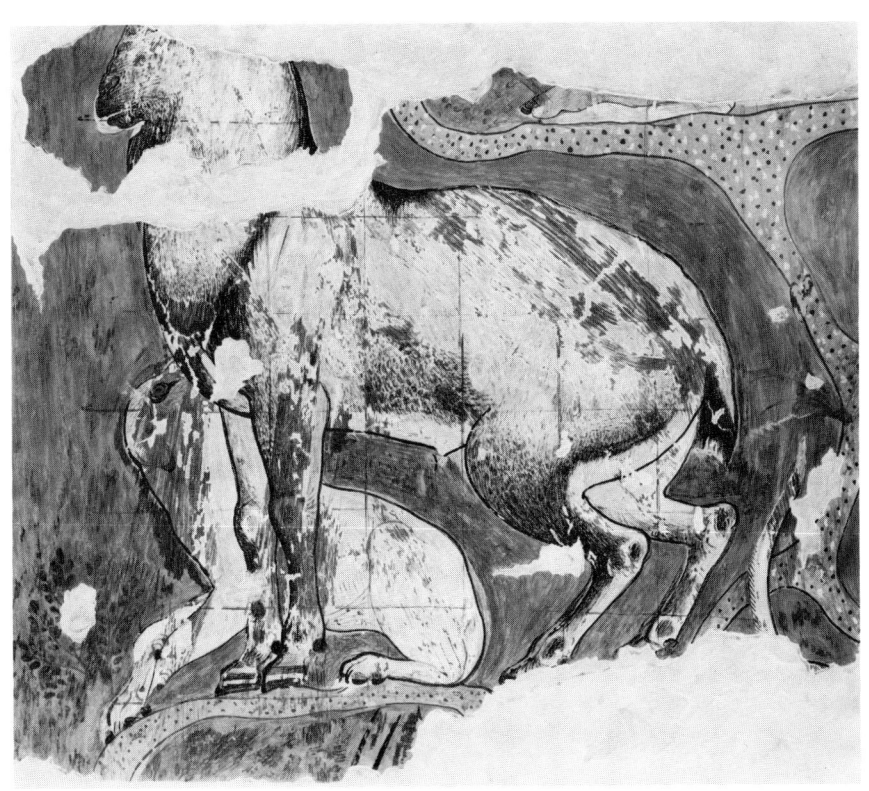

99

RELIEF CARVINGS
IN THE TOMB
OF RAMOSE,
THEBES *XVIII Dynasty*
Above UNFINISHED
RELIEF (SHOWING
MEASURED DRAWING
AND FIRST CUTTING)
Opposite DETAIL OF
FIGURE OF AN
OFFERING-BEARER

The artists who decorated the large tomb-chapel of the vizier Ramose worked with superb craftsmanship and followed all the accepted rules of figure drawing. Ramose was the chief minister of King Amenhotep III, the most magnificent monarch of the Age of Empire. The vizier lived on into the next reign, but the decoration of his tomb was never completed. One wall of its spacious hall was painted, and two other walls were adorned with delicate carvings in low relief, mostly elegant figures of Ramose and his relations.

A look at the unfinished reliefs shows how the wall was ruled in squares to make sure that the figures would be drawn in fault-less proportions. The sculptor then chiseled along the lines of the drawing and smoothed his carving to the perfection and refine-ment of the figure at the right—an offering-bearer with a bunch of papyrus.

100

For all their perfection, the carvings in the tomb of Ramose
seem curiously lifeless. The tomb-chapel of his contemporary,
the queen's steward Kheruef, gives us a far more exciting picture

of the splendor and pageantry of the age. This tomb also was un-usually large, befitting a man of high rank, and was decorated with reliefs.

The broad pillared hall of the tomb, carved out of the lime-stone hillside, was entered through a porch from a courtyard open to the sky. Stepping into the porch, we find ourselves in the midst of the ancient jubilee festival, celebrated by the Egyptians to renew the youth of their reigning king. All along the wall, on either side of the doorway into the hall, we can follow the carvings of two jubilee celebrations, complete with dancing, sing-ing, and games. Here the king himself appears, Amenhotep III, protected on his throne by the Horus falcon and holding in his right hand the "ankh," the hieroglyphic sign of life.

This king, all-powerful ruler of Egypt and the empire, was a very different figure from his predecessors, warrior kings like Thutmose III. Amenhotep felt no call to be a warrior, leading his armies forth to defend, and extend, the borders of the empire. Egypt and her allies abroad seemed secure from attack, and rich tribute was pouring into Thebes. The king could live a life of ease and pleasure, and above all, he could show his devotion to Amon-Re, the king of the gods, who had granted the Egyptians victory in war and blessed the land with such prosperity.

RELIEF CARVINGS
IN THE TOMB OF
KHERUEF, THEBES
XVIII Dynasty
Opposite KING
AMENHOTEP III
Below DANCERS
IN THE JUBILEE
CELEBRATION

KING AMENHOTEP III AND QUEEN TIY *XVIII Dynasty*

The Southern Sanctuary

The power and wealth of the Egyptian empire and its ruler demanded that royal statues and temples should be made on a mighty scale, rivaling the works of the pyramid builders. Amenhotep III looked back to those ancient times of Egypt's greatest glory, and in such colossal sculptures as this statue of the king and his "Great Royal Wife" we see his attempt to revive the old monumental art.

With the best artists in Egypt at his service, and with a force of laborers swelled by prisoners of war from distant lands, the king could undertake vast building schemes for the glory of Amon. He was not content to enrich the temple at Karnak. Amenhotep considered himself the son of Amon and resolved to build in Thebes a new and splendid house for Amon, the god's

SYRIANS BRINGING
GIFTS AT THE
ACCESSION OF
AMENHOTEP III
*Wall painting from
the tomb of
Sebenkhotep,
Chief Treasurer
Thebes,
XVIII Dynasty*

105

LUXOR TEMPLE (LOOKING SOUTH DOWN THE
CORRIDOR FROM THE COURT OF RAMESSES II)

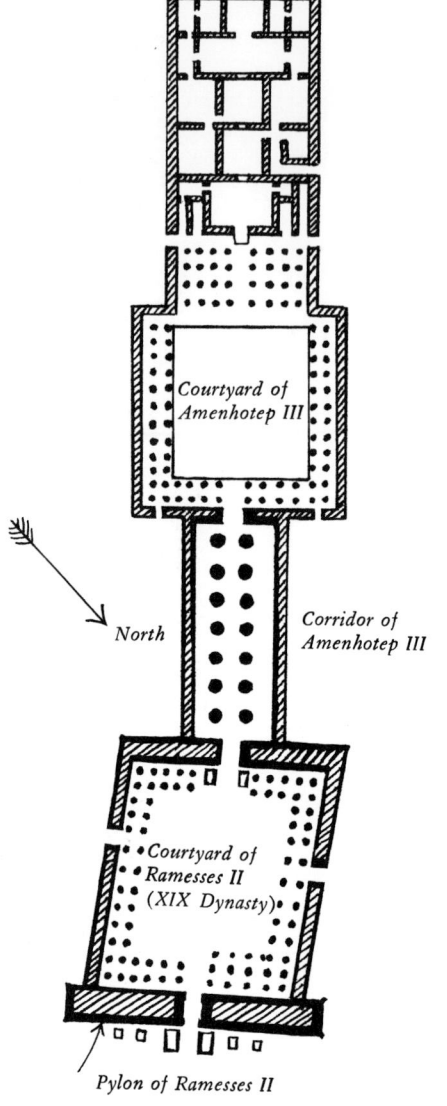

*Courtyard of
Amenhotep III*

North

*Corridor of
Amenhotep III*

*Courtyard of
Ramesses II
(XIX Dynasty)*

Pylon of Ramesses II

PLAN OF THE
LUXOR TEMPLE

wife Mut, and their child Khonsu, god of the moon. The king
chose a site by the river, probably the place of an older sanctuary,
and today we can still see his building there, magnificent even
in its ruin. We know it as the Luxor Temple; to the king and his
people it was the Southern Sanctuary.

106

We enter the temple through a huge gateway and courtyard that were added to the building by King Ramesses II. Immense seated statues of this later king flank the entrance to the long columned corridor, built by Amenhotep III as a processional avenue to the forecourt of the god's house. Every year, at the Festival of

LUXOR TEMPLE
(LOOKING NORTH FROM
THE COURT OF
AMENHOTEP III
TO THE GATEWAY PYLON
OF RAMESSES II)

107

Opet, a majestic and joyful procession would pass this way, bringing Amon of Karnak to visit his Southern Sanctuary, as at the Feast of the Valley he visited the temples and tombs of the western shore.

The Festival of Opet was in summer, when the Nile was high and the valley fields were under water. The farmers flocked to Thebes from miles around to celebrate the holiday with the people of the town. Only the priests might enter the sacred precincts of the temples, but when the barks of the three gods—Amon, Mut, and Khonsu—were carried forth from the Temple of Karnak, the people crowded to see them. The boat of each god was placed on a barge and towed to the Southern Sanctuary, either going up the Nile or along a canal that ran parallel to the

LUXOR TEMPLE
(THE COURTYARD
OF AMENHOTEP III)

river. Throngs of people, watching from the water's edge, greeted the barks of the gods with dancing and drumming and song. They might even catch a glimpse of the king at the journey's end. Amenhotep, in a golden chariot, led the procession down the corridor to the temple court, followed by the white-robed priests with the barks of the gods, the lines of offering-bearers, and the cattle for sacrifice.

Across the sunlit temple court the procession moved against a background of columns shaped like bundles of papyrus stems. Massive yet never clumsy, these columns recalled the ancient architecture of King Zoser at Sakkara, where the shapes of growing things were first translated into building stone. A lofty entrance hall beyond the court led to the small intimate rooms of the god's house, one of which was adorned with reliefs showing the miraculous birth of the king as the son of Amon-Re. The

DECORATED OXEN
FOR SACRIFICE
*From reliefs of the
Opet procession in
the Luxor Temple*

109

barks of the three gods were set down in three sanctuaries, also richly decorated, and there they rested until the ten-day feast was over and Amon and his family were carried back to their northern home.

These festivals at Thebes were triumphs for Amenhotep III and the god he served, but as the king grew older, the priests of Karnak knew that the rule of Amon was already challenged by a bitter enemy—the king's own son and heir to the throne.

Within a few years the god's power was shattered. Even in Thebes, the worship of Amon was forbidden; his temples were closed, and the names of the god and the king who had loved him were hacked out of the reliefs on the walls. Men were commanded to worship one god alone, the ancient sun-god called the Aten, who gave life to the land and the people.

During the last years of Amenhotep III his son may have reigned beside him as co-ruler, under the name of Amenhotep IV. Not content with sweeping away the old faith and worship of the people, the young man began a revolution in their art; and as a final break with the past, he moved the capital down the Nile to a new city of his own, founded in a place called Amarna today, and known to him as "The Horizon of the Aten." He changed his name, Amenhotep, which meant "Amon is satisfied," to Akhenaten, "Serviceable to the Aten," and could at last devote himself to the worship of his god and to the fulfillment of his dreams of new life and new art.

CARNELIAN PLAQUE FROM
BRACELET OR ANKLET
(CARVING OF AMENHOTEP III
ENTHRONED, HIS DAUGHTERS
OFFERING PALM BRANCHES
SYMBOLIC OF LONG LIFE)
XVIII Dynasty
(*Compare relief on page 102*)

V

Akhenaten's Revolution

New Art at
the King's Command

This carving of the king and queen and one of their daughters worshiping the Aten shows us Akhenaten's strange new art and his daring break with old, revered traditions.

The king, larger than the other figures, is almost a caricature of a man and has none of the majesty of kingship. The god he worships is not represented by a human figure, or even a figure with the head of an animal. The Aten is the disk of the sun with its life-giving rays ending in tiny hands that hold out the "ankh," the sign of life, to the king and queen. Instead of a burnt sacrifice, an offering of lotus flowers is placed before the god, and his worship is in the open air, not in a dark and mysterious temple sanctuary. Here is no mystery, no darkness, for the Aten is the god of light, and in his beams all things are revealed and the truth about all things made known.

It was the king's devotion to truth that made him demand to be portrayed as he was, lean-faced and weak in body. Yet

Opposite
KING AKHENATEN
AND HIS FAMILY
WORSHIPING
*Relief carving
from Amarna
XVIII Dynasty*

DETAIL OF A RELIEF
IN THE AMARNA STYLE
*In the tomb of Ramose,
Thebes, XVIII Dynasty*

he was still to be worshiped as god-king. In fact, Akhenaten considered himself an even greater god than the kings of the past, for they had shared their place with a host of other deities. Now the old gods were swept away by the one supreme Aten. The king was the son of the god, and the people could worship the Aten only through him. They owed the king their reverence and their prayers, and all his subjects must bow like slaves before him.

The bowing figures above, typical of the new art, appear on the wall of a Theban tomb we have already seen—the large unfinished tomb of the vizier Ramose. Living on after the death of Amenhotep III, Ramose wisely changed the style of the decoration in his tomb to fit the new king's ideas. He even included a carving of Akhenaten and the queen under the rays of the Aten, a favorite theme in the tombs of the king's officials and courtiers at Amarna.

The artists of Amarna were closely supervised by the king. His temples and palaces needed lavish schemes of decoration which the hard-worked sculptors carried out in "sunk relief," the traditional method for adorning the outside walls of buildings. Instead of the figures being raised above the background, they were carved below it. This technique not only brought quick results, but the deeply cut outlines of the figures made a vivid and dramatic effect of light and shade on the sunlit walls.

Two heads of the king, finely carved in sunk relief, might have served as models for apprentices to copy. Many of the

SCULPTOR'S
TRIAL PIECE
From Amarna
XVIII Dynasty

artists who accompanied Akhenaten to his new city must have been young and inexperienced, not yet rooted in the habits and conventions of the old art. The king taught them that the new art must first of all be truthful, revealing the world and its people as they appeared by the light of the sun, not in the rigid forms hallowed by long usage.

Freed from old rules, the artists were also faced with startling new subject matter. The happy life of the royal family was to be made public. They could be shown driving about town in their chariot, eating roast fowl at the family table, or simply enjoying each other's company. In this small unfinished statue the king kisses one of his little daughters, perched on his knee, and the tenderness of his gesture is perfectly caught by the sculptor.

If at first the artists created caricatures in their zeal to please the king, the quest for truth in art led them later to make some wonderful portraits in which the people of the court rise up before us, from worn old officials to the young princesses.

Love of nature was a rule of life at Amarna, an essential part of the joyful outdoor worship of the Aten. The paintings on the walls and floors of royal palaces and rich men's houses

Left UNFINISHED STATUE
OF KING AKHENATEN
WITH A CHILD ON HIS KNEE
Right HEAD OF
AKHENATEN'S ELDEST
DAUGHTER *Forming the lid
of an alabaster jar for use
in her tomb, XVIII Dynasty*

117

were a reflection of the sunlit world outside—the trees, birds, and flowers of the city's many gardens. It was not hard for the painters of these pictures to follow the king's commands. They had a long tradition of drawing animals with grace and freedom, and the picture of ducks flying over a thicket of papyrus

118

is a direct descendant of the marsh scenes in painted tombs of many years before.

Small works of art give us an intimate glimpse of court life in Akhenaten's new city. A carved and colored ivory panel, on the lid of a wooden chest, shows the boy king who was Akhenaten's successor and spent his childhood at Amarna. He stands with his little queen in a garden pavilion, entwined with garlands and grapevines, and she offers him a bunch of flowers.

This small masterpiece is only one among the many treasures belonging to the boy king. The young Tutankhamen is more famous today than any other Egyptian king. He brought a swift end to Akhenaten's revolution, but his fame arises not from the actions of his short life but from the incredible riches discovered in his tomb.

119

FRESCO PAINTING
OF DUCKS AND
PAPYRUS *From
Amarna
XVIII Dynasty*

IVORY STATUETTE
OF A GAZELLE
XVIII Dynasty

Treasures of the Young King

Tutankhamen's coronation at the ancient temple of Karnak
was the sign of Amon's return to power and the doom of
Akhenaten's dreams. The people were free at last to worship
their old gods. Neglected temples were reopened and artists put
to work making new sacred statues and new relief carvings.
Tutankhamen was proud of being the king who ''spent his life
making images of the gods.''

The king's throne, magnificently plated with gold, was probably made at Amarna before Tutankhamen moved the capital
from Akhenaten's new city back to Thebes, the city of Amon.
The picture on the back panel of the throne is in the style of
the new art. The Aten sun-disk stretches out its small hands

FROM THE TOMB
OF TUTANKHAMEN:
Above DETAIL OF
BACK OF THRONE
Opposite GOLD MASK
OF THE MUMMY
XVIII Dynasty

to Tutankhamen and his queen, as he sits enthroned and she anoints him with perfume. Enriched with silver and colored inlays, the scene has the brilliance of jewelry.

Perhaps a sculptor from Amarna, trained to be truthful in his art, made the sensitive portrait of Tutankhamen in royal regalia. This living image, worked in gold, was the mask placed over the head of the young king before he was laid

in his tomb. Tutankhamen died before he was twenty, after a reign of only nine years. Three thousand years were to pass before his small tomb was discovered in the Valley of the Kings at Thebes and all the riches of a king's burial were revealed.

In the sealed, underground tomb the great stone coffin of Tutankhamen was enclosed within four rectangular gilded shrines. Inside the stone sarcophagus were three more coffins, made in the shape of the king's body and fitting tightly, one within the other. The first two were of wood covered with gold leaf; the third one, which held the king's body, was made of solid gold and precious stones.

When we look at this innermost coffin, with the features of the boy king molded in gold, we see Tutankhamen transfigured into an image of calm, peace, and infinite dignity. He has become the embodiment of Osiris, the god of the underworld. He wears the beard of Osiris and carries the god's symbols, the crook and the flail. For added protection, the vulture- and cobra-goddesses enfold him with their wings, golden wings in which every feather is inlaid with jeweled color.

Tutankhamen is no longer an individual, a lonely boy set on the throne. He is the Pharaoh, the god-king who will join the other gods in everlasting life.

Even the things he had used in his lifetime contributed to this vision of him as the mighty Pharaoh, successor of the royal empire builders. On the footstool of one of his thrones are the figures of nine bound prisoners, symbolizing the nine traditional enemies of Egypt to be trodden beneath his feet. A ceremonial

FROM THE TOMB
OF TUTANKHAMEN:
Opposite UPPER PART
OF THE GOLD COFFIN
Below FOOTSTOOL
OF A THRONE

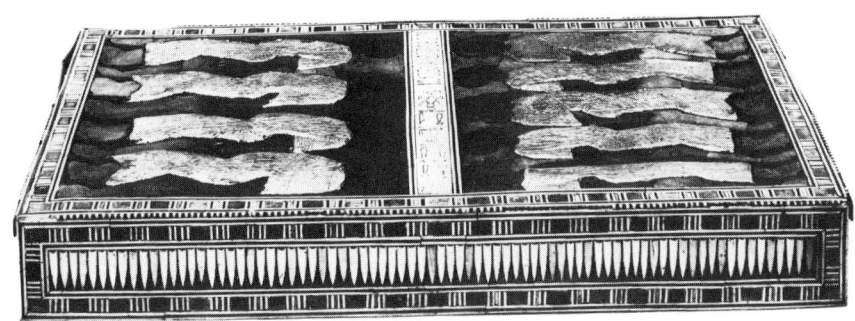

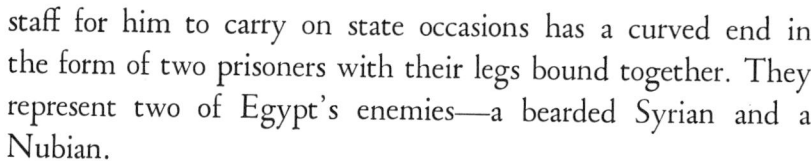

staff for him to carry on state occasions has a curved end in the form of two prisoners with their legs bound together. They represent two of Egypt's enemies—a bearded Syrian and a Nubian.

One of the most exciting works of art in all the king's treasure is a small wooden chest with no gold or jewels in its making. Its whole surface is covered with miniature paintings by the hand of a master artist. Two scenes on the lid show the Pharaoh as a huntsman, slaying lions, desert antelopes, and wild asses. At the ends of the box the king is pictured as a sphinx, crushing his enemies beneath his paws, and on the sides he charges into battle in a chariot drawn by prancing plumed horses. His enemies fall before him in a tangle of tumbling bodies and faces contorted with pain—Syrians on one side and Nubians on the other.

PAINTED CHEST
OF TUTANKHAMEN

Left LOWER END OF
TUTANKHAMEN'S
CEREMONIAL
WALKING STICK
Right TUTANKHAMEN'S
FOLDING STOOL
(*Probably made
in Nubia*)

NUBIAN BATTLE *From the painted chest*

SYRIAN BATTLE
*From Tutankhamen's
painted chest*

These wonderful pictures of the fighting Pharaoh were far from the truth. The delicate young king had never ridden to victory in battle, and the Egyptian empire, neglected by Akhenaten, was hard pressed by enemies. It was not until the beginning of the Nineteenth Dynasty, thirty years after Tutankhamen's death, that the kings of Egypt once more became conquerors and were proud to leave a record of their deeds, in words and pictures, for all to see.

The intimacy of Akhenaten's art was not for them; they chose the colossal and majestic art of the distant past to glorify themselves and their victories. Yet the new freedom, energy, and drama that we see in the battle paintings of the boy king were part of the heritage of his successors. The tiny delicate pictures on Tutankhamen's chest were forerunners of vast battle scenes that covered whole walls with hundreds of struggling figures, dominated always by the mighty form of the victorious Pharaoh.

126

VI The Victorious Pharaohs

The Walls of Karnak

The warrior Pharaoh, Seti I, stormed from end to end of the Egyptian empire, beating back the invaders who harried its borders. In the West, he crushed the Libyans, the desert people of North Africa who threatened the rich land of the delta. In Syria the dreaded Hittites were put to flight and tried in vain to hold the walled city of Kadesh against the onslaught of Egyptian power.

The saga of Seti's battles and his triumphal homecoming with prisoners of war is told in these reliefs at Karnak, carved on the outer wall of the great hypostyle hall. When the morning sunlight slants across the wall, the figures spring to life. Ink-black shadows fill the deep outlines of the sunk relief and sharply define the flaring nostrils and wide eyes of the horses, the hollow cheeks of captives, and the gesture of the terrified herdsman fleeing with his cattle before the attackers of Kadesh.

RELIEFS ON THE
NORTH WALL OF
THE HYPOSTYLE
HALL, KARNAK:
Above BATTLE AT
KADESH (*See
detail on page 14*)
XIX Dynasty

128

FLEEING HERDSMAN *Detail of top right corner of the relief opposite*

KING SETI I
WITH PRISONERS
OF WAR

CENTRAL AISLE OF THE HYPOSTYLE HALL, KARNAK *XIX Dynasty*

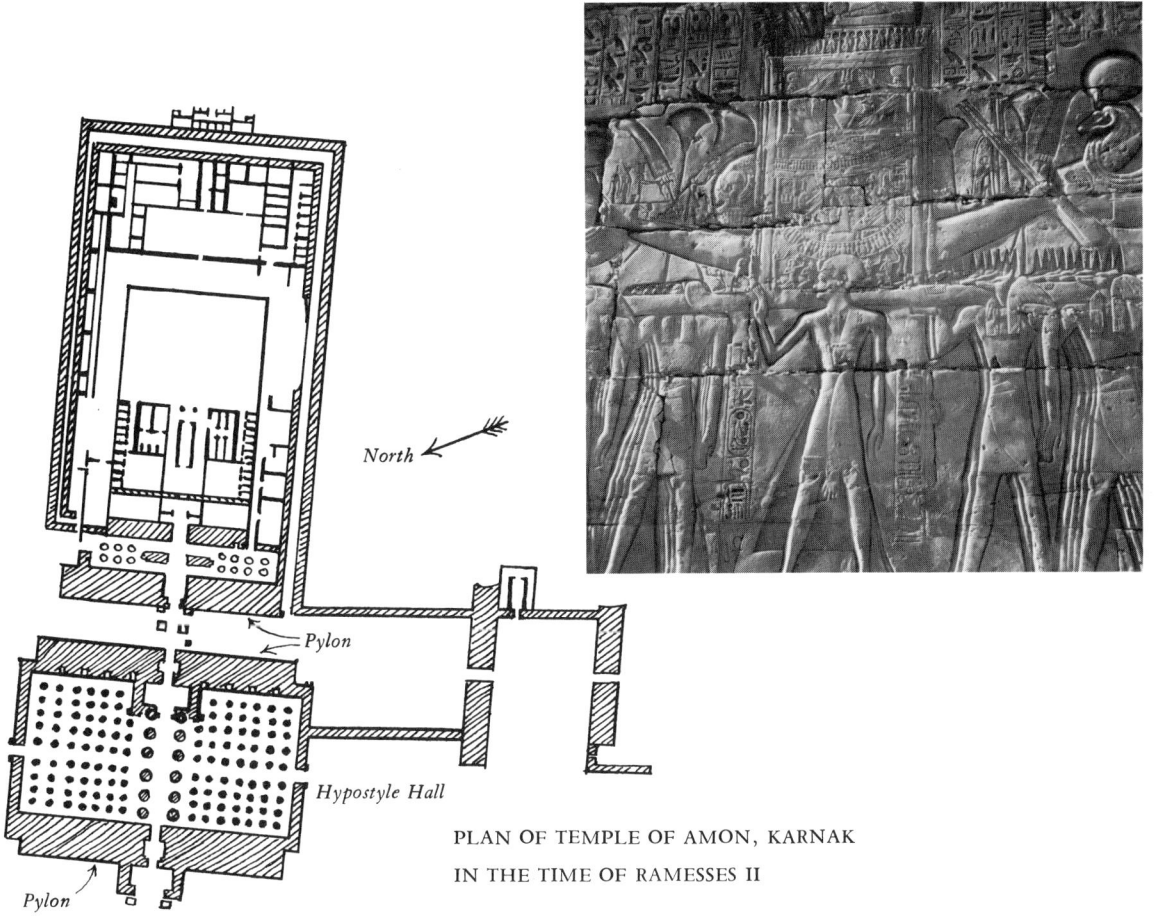

North

Pylon

Hypostyle Hall

Pylon

PLAN OF TEMPLE OF AMON, KARNAK
IN THE TIME OF RAMESSES II

Seti's thank offering to Amon for these victories in battle was the great hypostyle hall itself. No one had ever dared to build a hall so vast. The huge columns to support the roof are crowded together like giant forest trees, their bulbous trunks covered with hieroglyphs and incised figures. One hundred and thirty-four columns stand in a space of more than an acre. Far away between them we catch narrow glimpses of the walls, spread with rich carvings of kings and gods and processions of priests, once painted in vivid color.

Above SACRED
BARK OF AMON
CARRIED IN
PROCESSION
*From a relief in
the Hypostyle Hall,
Karnak
XIX Dynasty*

131

The hall was a place for processions, and the people of Thebes could come here to watch them. The days of festival, when the sacred barks of the gods would be carried through the hall, are commemorated in the reliefs on the walls. We see the bark of Amon borne by priests wearing the masks of hawks and jackals. A decorated shrine hides the statue of the god, and at the prow and stern of his boat are the heads of his sacred rams.

These reliefs were carved by the artists of Ramesses II, the son and successor of Seti. Ramesses appears on the same wall, kneeling before Amon to receive the emblems of his royal office. Humble as he seems before the king of the gods, Ramesses was obsessed by his own glory. His subjects were never allowed to forget the greatness of their king. Up the Nile valley, from the delta to Aswan and distant Nubia, he built a succession of temples, always adorned with gigantic statues of himself, but of all his works none is more famous than the Nubian temple of Abu Simbel.

KING RAMESSES II RECEIVING
THE EMBLEMS OF OFFICE
FROM THE GOD AMON
(WITH THE GODDESS MUT
IN ATTENDANCE)
*Relief in the Hypostyle Hall,
Karnak XIX Dynasty*

132

To the Glory of Ramesses

The temple at Abu Simbel, with its four colossal statues of Ramesses II gazing eastward across the river, was an everlasting reminder to the rebellious Nubians of the strength and glory of their overlord, the Pharaoh of Egypt.

Since the days of the pyramid builders, the Egyptians had traded with the people of Nubia and built forts and temples along the rocky upper reaches of the Nile above Aswan. Ramesses himself built other Nubian temples, but Abu Simbel was unique. Dedicated to the god of the rising sun, Re-Harakhty, the temple was a part of both the earth and sky. The sloping hillside formed its façade, and the statues were carved from the living rock. The temple hall and sanctuary were cut deep into the hill, but at certain seasons the first beams of the sun would strike directly through the doorway. Then the dark

Above
THE GREAT TEMPLE
AT ABU SIMBEL
XIX Dynasty
(BEFORE THE TEMPLE
WAS MOVED TO
ITS PRESENT
HIGHER SITE, DUE TO
THE BUILDING OF
THE HIGH DAM)

*On the façade of
the Great Temple,
Abu Simbel*

sanctuary would be filled with light, revealing the statues of Re and Amon, Ptah the creator-god, and Ramesses the king.

The great temple shared the hillside with a smaller one, built by Ramesses for his queen, Nefertari, and dedicated to Hathor. On its façade were four standing statues of the king

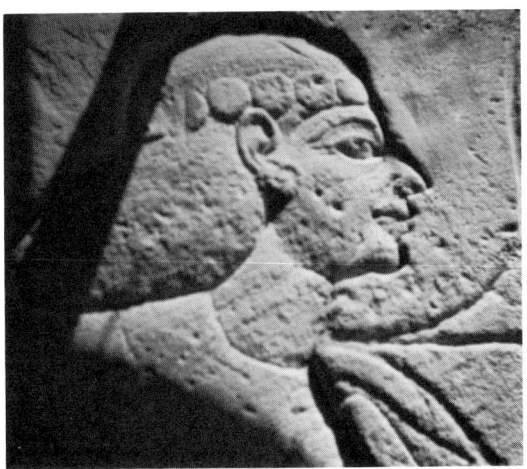

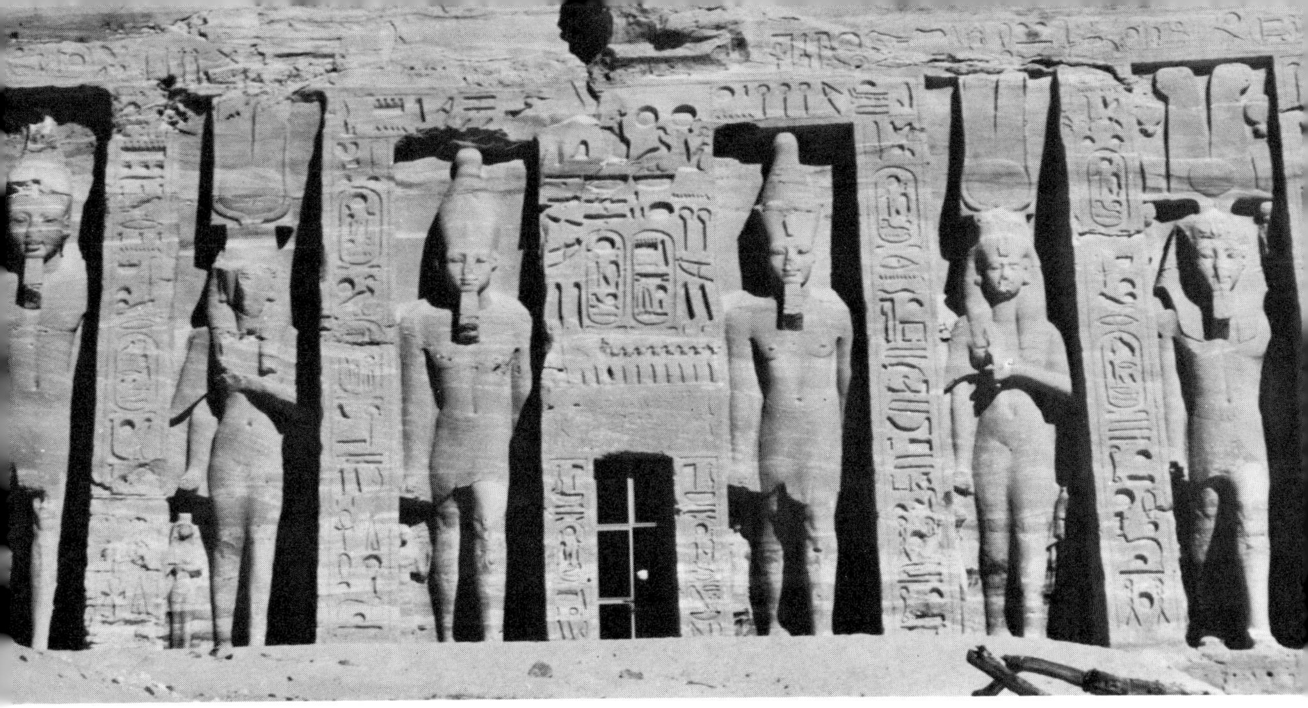

FAÇADE OF THE TEMPLE OF HATHOR, ABU SIMBEL
XIX Dynasty

and two of the queen, gentle figures compared with the brutal strength of the four seated giants.

The great temple glorified the king as conqueror. On the footstools of the statues are carvings of bound prisoners. Rough in workmanship, they are vivid in their delineation of Syrians and Nubians, Libyans and Hittites, many of whom probably labored on the building of the temple.

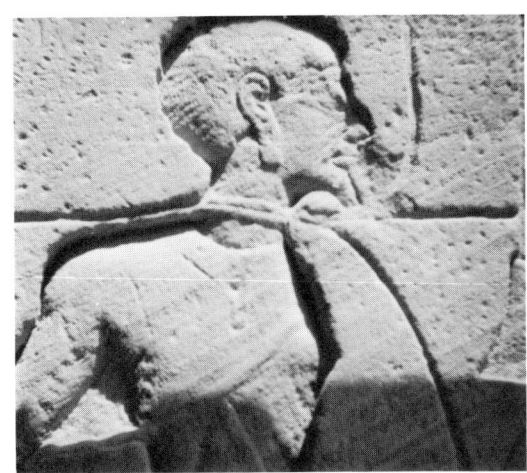

HITTITE AND SYRIAN *Carvings on the façade of the Great Temple, Abu Simbel*

HALL OF THE
GREAT TEMPLE,
ABU SIMBEL

Through the doorway between the statues we pass from the
glare of the desert sun into the mysterious dimness of the temple hall. Eight rock-hewn figures of the king rise to the painted

136

roof and form an avenue, leading to a smaller hall and to the sanctuary beyond. Narrow doorways at the sides open into little chambers for treasures and offerings, and everywhere the warm brown walls are rich with reliefs, some still with traces of color. Over and over again we see tall figures of the king before the gods, but in the great hall pride of place is given to his triumphs in war, and above all, to the famous battle of Kadesh.

Ramesses' courage in that battle was never forgotten. Like his father, Seti, he advanced into Syria against the Hittites, but near Kadesh he fell into an enemy ambush. His men were routed, and the Pharaoh was surrounded by the Hittite chariots. Almost singlehanded, Ramesses fought his way out of the trap. Fresh Egyptian forces raced to his rescue, and with the king at their head, they turned the tide of battle.

THE KING SMITING ENEMY PRISONERS: *Left* KING NARMER *I Dynasty Right* KING RAMESSES II *From a relief in the hall of the Great Temple, Abu Simbel XIX Dynasty*

137

THE BATTLE OF
KADESH
*From a relief in
the Ramesseum,
the temple of
Ramesses II,
Thebes
XIX Dynasty*

Ramesses was welcomed home as a hero, and he commanded the epic story of the battle to be carved on his temples throughout the land. During his long reign the battle of Kadesh was unrolled across huge stretches of temple walls. One of the most exciting pictures of it was in the king's mortuary temple, on the west bank of the Nile at Thebes.

138

There we can see the battle in all its fury before the walled city of Kadesh and the waters of the River Orontes. A giant-sized Ramesses charges in his chariot, crushing the enemy beneath the hoofs of his horses and driving them panic-stricken into the river to struggle and drown.

Many of the relief carvings in this temple were copied by

PYLON OF THE
TEMPLE OF KING
RAMESSES III
AT MEDINET HABU,
THEBES
XX Dynasty

the artists of Ramesses III and used in the decoration of his own temple close by. Ramesses III came to the throne thirty or forty years after the death of his great predecessor, and he also left a proud record of victory over the enemies of Egypt. Carved along the northern wall of his temple are reliefs of fierce battles on land and sea against invasions by the Libyans and the "Sea Peoples," and tall figures of the king smiting enemy prisoners adorn the front of the gateway pylon. But the carvings on the back of the pylon tell a different story. Here we see the king as a sportsman in the royal sport of hunting.

Almost leaping from his chariot, Ramesses plunges into the reedbeds by the river after wild bulls. Two of the great beasts have fallen, transfixed by arrows. A third collapses in the rushes at the water's edge, its legs giving way, its mouth open and gasping. Below the king's chariot his archers hasten after him, and above, in the open desert, the Pharaoh appears again, drawing his bow against herds of fleeing antelope and wild

140

HUNTING SCENE *Relief carved on the back of the pylon, Temple of Ramesses III, Medinet Habu, Thebes, XX Dynasty*

asses. All the hunting scenes, carved and painted by Egyptian artists for centuries past, seem to lead up to this superb picture, which not only glorifies the king but the noble animals he hunted and the fair land he shared with them.

Hidden from the front of the temple, the hunting scene faced a little palace, a place where the king could rest from affairs of state. A window of the palace opened onto the first courtyard of the temple and gave the king a view of the ceremonies there. At the joyful Feast of the Valley he would come

142

forth to greet the barks of the Theban gods when they moved in procession to the temple sanctuary.

RESTORED
FOUNDATIONS OF
THE PALACE AT
MEDINET HABU
(THRONE ROOM AT
THE LEFT WITH SMALL
APARTMENTS BEHIND)

The kings now had their capital at Tanis in the delta, and Thebes was no longer the chief city of the Two Lands; but it was still the holy town of Amon and its western shore the place for royal burial. The Pharaohs built their mortuary temples along the desert's edge, and their tombs lay westward, tunneled deep into the rock in the desolate Valley of the Kings.

Like the pyramid builders of old, the Pharaohs sought to make their burials safe from robbers and to preserve their mortal bodies from decay. The tombs of the great rulers of the Eighteenth, Nineteenth, and Twentieth dynasties were far bigger and more elaborate than the four small rooms that held the treasures of the boy Tutankhamen. The kings' burial chambers were guarded by secret entries, open pits, and blind branching alleys, and the walls and ceilings of the rock-hewn rooms and passageways were covered with drawings, paintings, and reliefs.

A single tomb took years to make and decorate, and some were never finished. Stonecutters and sculptors, scribes and painters worked their whole lives through in this royal city of the dead. These were the "Servants in the Place of Truth."

143

WRESTLERS *From
reliefs in the first
courtyard of the
temple, Medinet Habu*

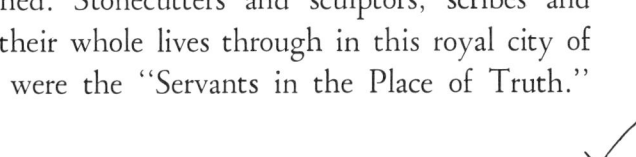

FOUNDATIONS OF THE
VILLAGE OF THE CRAFTSMEN
Deir el Medineh, Thebes

Servants in the Place of Truth

The Place of Truth, home of the artists and craftsmen of the royal tombs, lay in a hollow of the brown, barren hills of the western shore. We can still see the foundations of the neat walled village, with houses crowded together along two narrow streets. The people who lived there could look out between the hills to the green fields of the river valley, but they were seldom allowed to leave their village, except to go over the mountain to the royal tombs.

In the small workshops of the village houses, boys would learn the crafts of their fathers. Master painters taught their sons how to draw figures in correct proportion with a firm sure line, and novice scribes would copy endless hieroglyphs, first on scraps of stone and finally on rolls of papyrus. Broken bits of limestone, scattered everywhere in the hills, were the notebooks of the scribes and painters, on which they kept their records or simply scribbled drawings for their own delight, after long days of labor in the tombs.

144

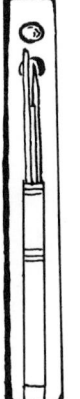

TOOLS OF THE SCRIBE:
PALETTES AND RUSH PENS

The biggest tomb they worked on in the Valley of the Kings was made for Seti I, the Pharaoh whose victories were carved on the sunlit walls of Karnak. In the long gloomy corridors of his tomb there was no memory of his triumphs on earth. The reliefs on the walls, beautifully carved and painted, described the king's journey with the sun-god Re through the terrible valley of the underworld to the kingdom of Osiris. The corridors of the tomb, descending into deeper and deeper darkness, were symbolic of that dark valley through which the king must pass, a nightmare world of rearing snakes, men without heads, lakes of fire, and hideous monsters guarding pits of doom.

Tall majestic figures of the king confronted the gods in the underworld—Osiris and his wife Isis, Hathor, and the jackal-headed Anubis; and on the vaulted ceiling of the burial chamber, far under the hill, the black night sky was painted, with the constellations in the form of men and beasts.

FLAKE OF LIMESTONE
WITH SKETCH OF
A HUNTING SCENE

145

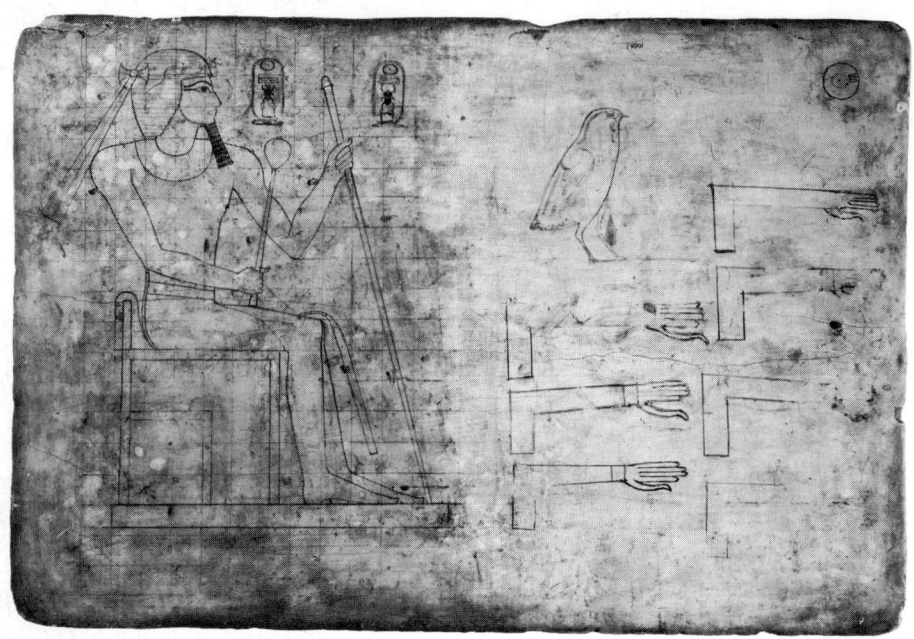

Learned scribes must have planned and superintended the work on Seti's tomb, making sure the drawings were correct before the sculptors carved them in relief. The work was never finished. Some of the figures were left as outline drawings, and we can see how the draftsman's sketches were first made on the wall in red paint and then drawn over, and sometimes altered, with firm black lines.

Manuscripts supplied the models for the pictures and hieroglyphic texts in the tomb. *The Book of What Is in the Underworld* and *The Book of Gates* described the dangers of the dead man's journey and how they could be conquered, while *The Litany of Re* was written in praise of the sun-god, the king's companion in the dark valley. Copies of these books, and of the ancient *Book of the Dead,* were probably made by the scribes and their pupils in the Place of Truth.

TOMB OF KING SETI I, THEBES: CEILING OF THE BURIAL CHAMBER (SHOWING NORTHERN CONSTELLATIONS WITH THE BULL AND DRIVER REPRESENTING THE GREAT BEAR) *XIX Dynasty*

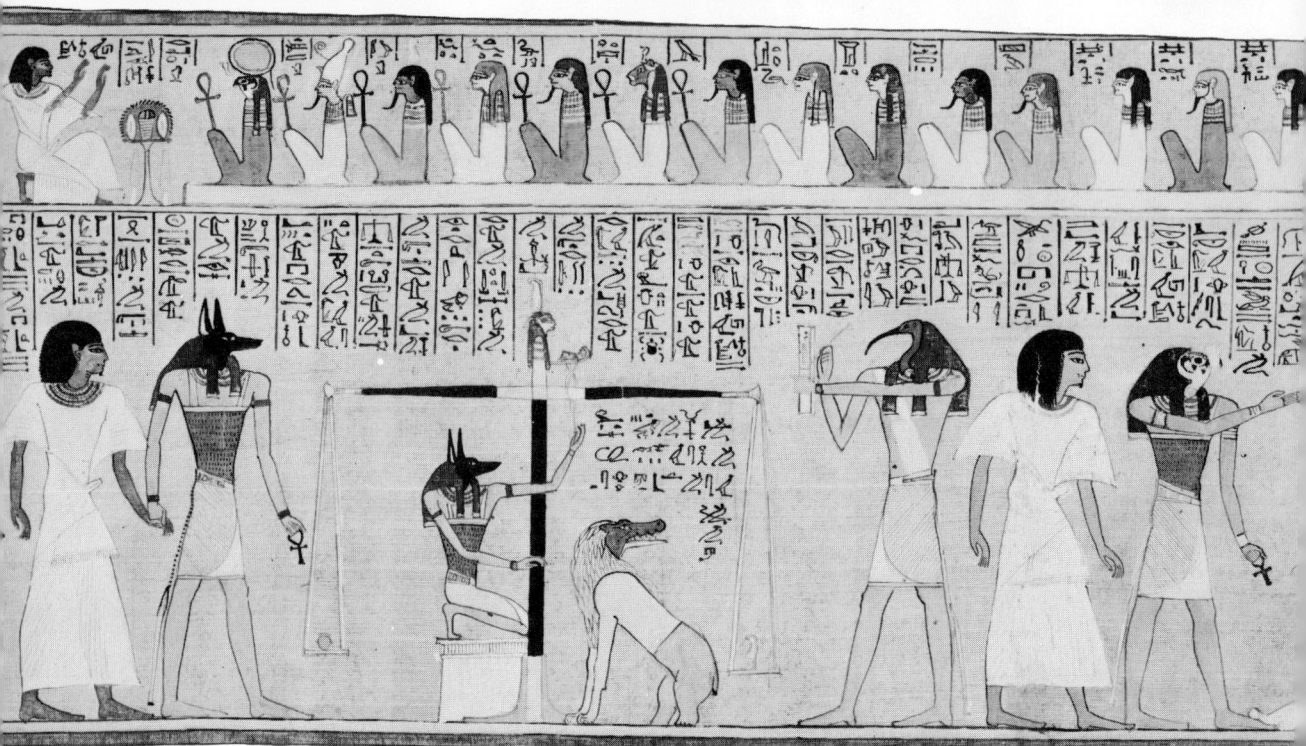

THE WEIGHING OF
THE HEART *From
the papyrus of
Hunefer, royal scribe
in the reign of Seti I
XIX Dynasty*

The Book of the Dead was a whole collection of writings intended to help the dead man achieve everlasting life. People were often buried with manuscripts of this book in their coffins. They ordered whatever chapters best suited their needs, and for wealthy customers scribes made copies with beautiful illustrations.

This delicate drawing from a fine manuscript of *The Book of the Dead* shows one of the worst ordeals the dead man had to undergo. His heart is being weighed in the balance against a feather representing Truth. If the heart is neither too heavy nor too light, he is worthy to enter the kingdom of Osiris. Anubis leads the man by the hand and watches over the weighing. Thoth, god of scribes, keeps the record, and the monster Amemt lurks beside the scale to devour the sinful heart if it should prove unworthy. He loses his prey, and at the right, Horus bids the dead man pass on into the presence of Osiris.

In another manuscript of the same book we see Horus leading the dead man before Osiris and telling the god of the underworld that the man's heart is true and has passed the test of the weighing. The man kneels and presents offerings to the god, who sits enthroned in a shrine with a roof made of living serpents rising from a stream of water. A lotus flower springs up before the god, and behind him stand Isis and her sister Nephthys, the mourners and protectors of the dead. The man is accepted by Osiris and at last he is ready to receive the final reward of everlasting life.

This reward was the hope of the Servants in the Place of Truth, who knew better than most men the importance of a proper burial to help the dead man reach Osiris' kingdom.

Up the steep rocky hillside behind their village they dug out their small tombs with little mud-brick chapels built in front. The painters decorated the burial chambers for themselves and their neighbors, using the same good colors that adorned the tombs of kings. The chapels have crumbled away, but the hill

THE DEAD MAN BEFORE OSIRIS *From The Book of the Dead of the scribe Ani*

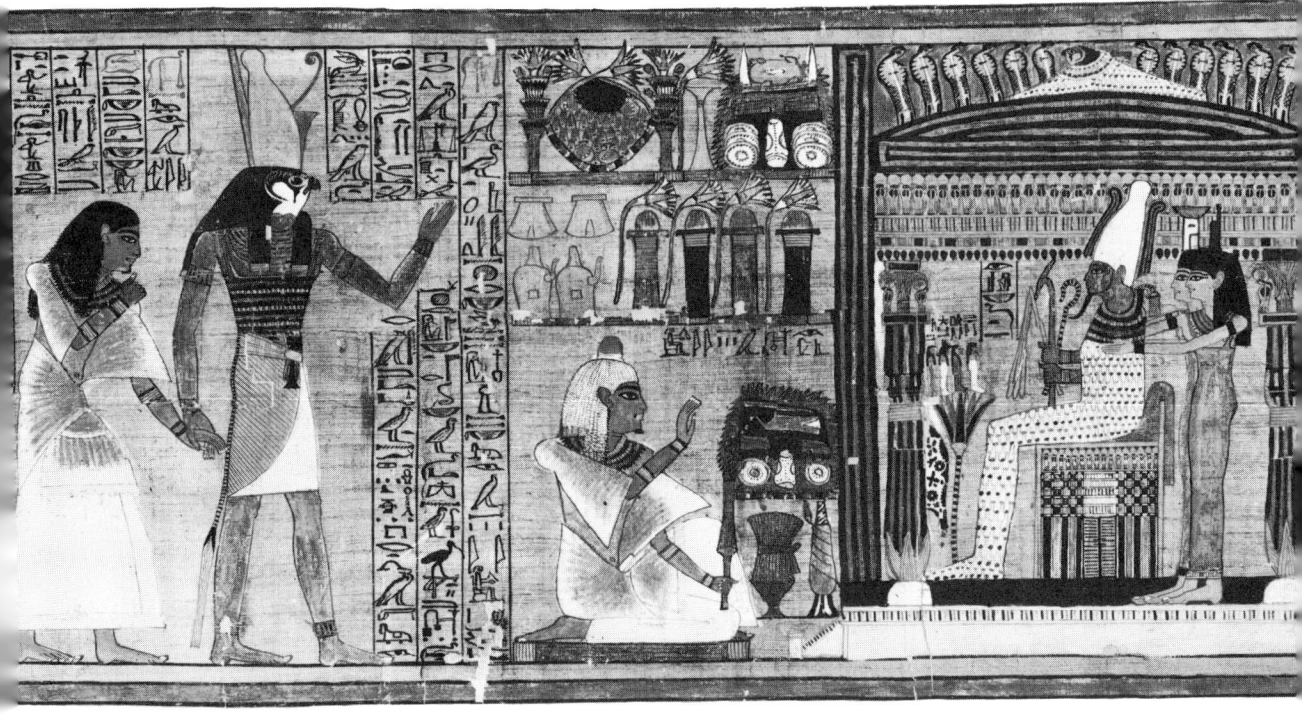

is pitted like a rabbit warren with the entrances to the tombs. Some are so tiny we must stoop to go in. In some the paintings are hastily daubed, or left unfinished with the figures in silhouette. One man wanted his tomb to be a bower of painted grapevines; another had his ceiling covered with hieroglyphic texts.

Sennedjem, one of the principal Servants in the Place of Truth, in the time of Ramesses II, made his tomb close to his house at the south end of the village. When we go from the scorching dry brightness outside into the small low burial chamber, we find it glowing with color. On walls and roof the large bold red-brown figures stand out in their white garments against a background of ocher yellow.

150

The pictures illustrate chapters of *The Book of the Dead,* and at the end of the room, framed in the arch of the roof, we see the reward of those who have passed the judgment of Osiris. Sennedjem and his wife are alive forever. Far from the barren wastes of the Place of Truth they plough and plant and reap in the Fields of Rushes, where trees are green and crops grow magically tall, refreshed by streams of never-failing water.

PAINTED TOMB
OF SENNEDJEM
Deir el Medineh,
Thebes
XIX Dynasty

The Enduring Art of Egypt

The story of ancient Egypt after the reign of Ramesses III tells of the land's long slow decline. We hear of bad harvests and famine when the Nile was low, and of the ruthless plundering of the royal tombs at Thebes. Then, at the end of the Twentieth Dynasty, King Ramesses XI surrendered his power to his vizier and to the High Priest of Amon, and for many years afterward the Two Lands were shared between two rulers —a High Priest at Thebes and a king at Tanis in the delta.

Egypt was reunited under later dynasties, but her ancient greatness and power were lost forever. Yet her art lived on. Egyptian arts and crafts had spread to the lands of the Eastern Mediterranean, where the Egyptians had traveled and traded and fought since the days of the pyramid builders. In the seventh century B.C., when Egypt was ruled by strong kings and enjoyed a revival of art, merchants from Greece were invited to settle in the delta and trade. They carried away from Egypt two ideas that were far more precious than shiploads of grain and fine linens and the small gay products of skilled craftsmen. The Greeks saw in Egypt, for the first time, great pillared

METALWORKERS
*From wall painting
in the tomb of
Rekhmire, Thebes
XVIII Dynasty*

152

temples and statues carved of stone. Greek art was built on these foundations.

In the centuries to come, when the classic art of Greece was known and honored by scholars, art lovers, and collectors throughout the western world, the art of Egypt was forgotten. Travelers might stare in awe at the pyramids and the Sphinx, but a shroud of mystery had settled over ancient Egypt. The meaning of the hieroglyphs was lost, and the disused temples were filled with drifts of sand. Village people made their homes in the empty tombs and blackened the paintings with the smoke of cooking fires.

Only in modern times did scholars begin to dig among the ruins. They solved the riddle of the hieroglyphs and found in the dry desert sand a wealth of art beyond imagining. Gradually the mists were cleared away, and the shadowy people of ancient Egypt, with their strange gods and fabled wisdom, came forth into the light of day.

They were practical people, to whom the statue of a king, even the work of an artist of genius, was as much a useful and necessary thing as a chair, a wine jar, or a chariot of war. The Egyptians had their feet firmly planted on the ground, the black earth of their own beloved river valley. Even when they ruled an empire, their land was to them the only place worth living in. They loved its blue sky and blue water, the fields and reedbeds, the animals of riverside and desert. Above all, they loved life and strove to conquer death.

The Pyramids of Giza stand as the greatest monuments to their love of life and battle against death, but the Egyptians speak to us today in all the things they made, both great and small. Through their enduring art they have won the everlasting life they longed for, thousands of years ago beside the Nile.

153

THE "ANKH," SIGN OF LIFE *From carving in the tomb of Kheruef, Thebes XVIII Dynasty*

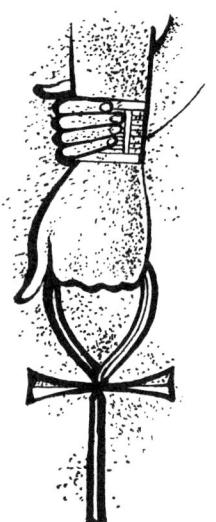

List of Illustrations

Photographs

FRONTISPIECE Wooden model of offering bearers from the tomb of Djehutynekht, Deir el Bersheh. XII Dynasty. (*Courtesy, Museum of Fine Arts, Boston, Harvard University and MFA Expedition*)

TITLE PAGE Ivory statuette of gazelle. XVIII Dynasty. (*The Metropolitan Museum of Art, Carnarvon Collection, Gift of Edward S. Harkness, 1926*)

PAGE

9 Group statuette of three brothers. From a tomb at Giza. V Dynasty. (*Courtesy, Museum of Fine Arts, Boston, Harvard University and MFA Expedition*)

10 The Great Sphinx, Giza. IV Dynasty. (*Photograph: the author*)

11 The Pyramids, Giza. IV Dynasty. (*Photograph: Marburg-Art Reference Bureau*)

12 Hypostyle Hall of the Temple of Amon, Karnak. XIX Dynasty. (*Photograph: Marburg-Art Reference Bureau*)

13 Relief carving of dancers in a tomb at Sakkara. (*Photograph: Lehnert and Landrock, Cairo*)

14 Battle scene. Detail from relief carving on the north wall of the Hypostyle Hall, Temple of Amon, Karnak. XIX Dynasty. (*Photograph by the Epigraphic Survey, The Oriental Institute, Luxor, Egypt*)

14 Wooden spoon in the form of a jackal and shell. XIX Dynasty. (*The British Museum*)

15 Pendant of inlaid gold. (See page 81) Papyrus scroll with animal drawings. XIX–XXII Dynasty. (*The British Museum*)

16 The Valley of the Queens, Thebes. (*Photograph: the author*)

17 View of the Nile at Thebes, looking to the western shore. (*Photograph by The Epigraphic Survey, The Oriental Institute, Luxor, Egypt*)

18 Ploughing and planting. Detail from a wall painting in the tomb of Nakht, Thebes. XVIII Dynasty. (*Photograph by Egyptian Expedition, The Metropolitan Museum of Art*)

19 Marsh scene. Wall painting from a tomb at Thebes. XVIII Dynasty. (*The British Museum*)

20 The Nile at Aswan. (*Photograph: Courtesy of the United Arab Republic Tourist Office, New York*)

21 "The Geese of Meidum." Wall painting from a tomb at Meidum. IV Dynasty. (*The Egyptian Museum, Cairo*) Small faience figure of roaring hippopotamus. About XII Dynasty. (*The British Museum*)

22 Nile ship. Copy of a wall painting in the tomb of Menna, Thebes. XVIII Dynasty. (*The Metropolitan Museum of Art*)

23 Union of the Two Lands. Carving on a statue of King Ramesses II, Luxor Temple. XIX Dynasty. (*Photograph: the author*)

24 Palette of King Narmer (back). I Dynasty. (*The Egyptian Museum, Cairo*)

25 Ivory statuette of a king. I Dynasty. (*The British Museum*)

26 Palette of King Narmer (front). I Dynasty. (*The Egyptian Museum, Cairo*)

27 Hieroglyphic inscription. (See page 51)

28 Hounds hunting gazelles. Black steatite disc inlaid with alabaster. I Dynasty. (*The Egyptian Museum, Cairo*)

29 Funerary stele of King Uadji. I Dynasty. The Louvre, Paris. (*Photograph: Marburg-Art Reference Bureau*)

31 Small schist statue of King Khasekhem. II Dynasty. (*The Egyptian Museum, Cairo*)

32 Stone figure of a frog. Predynastic period. (*The British Museum*)

33 Colossal head of King Userkaf. V Dynasty. (*The Egyptian Museum, Cairo*)

35 The Step Pyramid, Sakkara. III Dynasty. (*Photograph: Courtesy of the United Arab Republic Tourist Office, New York*)

37 The Step Pyramid of Sakkara from the south, with the columns of the small temple in the foreground. III Dynasty. (*Photograph: Marburg-Art Reference Bureau*)

38 Limestone statue of King Zoser. III Dynasty. (*The Egyptian Museum, Cairo*)

40 Pyramid of Khufu, Giza. IV Dynasty. (*Photograph: Art Reference Bureau*)

41 Colossal head of a king. End of III Dynasty. (*Courtesy of The Brooklyn Museum*)

44 The Great Sphinx, Giza. IV Dynasty. Valley Temple of the Pyramid of Khafre. IV Dynasty. (*Both photographs: the author*)

45 Pyramid of Khafre, Giza. IV Dynasty. (*Photograph: Marburg-Art Reference Bureau*)

46 Statue of King Khafre, Giza. IV Dynasty. The Egyptian Museum, Cairo. (*Photograph: Lehnert and Landrock, Cairo*)

47 Head of the statue of Khafre. (*The Egyptian Museum, Cairo*)

48 Pyramids of Khufu, Khafre and Menkaure, Giza. IV Dynasty. (*Photograph: Art Reference Bureau*)

49 Slate statue of King Menkaure and his queen. IV Dynasty. (*Courtesy, Museum of Fine Arts, Boston, Harvard University and MFA Expedition*)

50– Reproductions of furniture from the
51 tomb of Queen Hetep-heres I, Giza, IV Dynasty: armchair, carrying chair, and detail of hieroglyphic inscription on the back of the carrying chair. (*Courtesy, Museum of Fine Arts, Boston. Gift of Mrs. Charles Gaston Smith and group of friends*)

52 Offerings of cattle, geese and cranes. Relief carving in the tomb of Ptahhotep, Sakkara. V Dynasty. (*Photograph: Lehnert and Landrock, Cairo*)

54– Return from the hunt. Relief carving
55 in the tomb of Ptahhotep, Sakkara. V Dynasty. (*Photograph: Lehnert and Landrock, Cairo*)

56 Offering bearers. Relief in the tomb of Mereruka, Sakkara. VI Dynasty. (*Photograph: Courtesy of the Oriental Institute, University of Chicago*)

57 Statue of Mereruka in his tomb at Sakkara. VI Dynasty. (*Photograph: Courtesy of the Oriental Institute, University of Chicago*)

58 Statue of Bedjmes the shipbuilder. III Dynasty. (*The British Museum*)

59 Statue of Memy Sabu and his wife.

From a tomb at Giza. VI Dynasty. (*The Metropolitan Museum of Art, Rogers Fund, 1948*)

59 Statue of Katep and Hetep-heres. IV Dynasty. (*The British Museum*)

60 Seated scribe. IV Dynasty. (*The Egyptian Museum, Cairo*)

61 Portrait bust of the nobleman Ankhhaf. From his tomb at Giza. IV Dynasty. (*Courtesy, Museum of Fine Arts, Boston, Harvard University and MFA Expedition*)

62 Statuette of a potter at his wheel. From a tomb at Giza. VI Dynasty. (*Courtesy of the Oriental Institute, University of Chicago*)

63 Head of King Senwosret III. XII Dynasty. (*The Egyptian Museum, Cairo*)

64 King Mentuhotep. Relief carving from his mortuary temple at Deir el Bahri, Thebes. XI Dynasty. (*Courtesy, The Royal Scottish Museum, Edinburgh*)

66 King Senwosret III as a sphinx. XII Dynasty. (*The Metropolitan Museum of Art, Gift of Edward S. Harkness, 1916–17*)

67 Limestone statuette of kneeling man. XII Dynasty. (*The Metropolitan Museum of Art, Museum Excavations, 1913–14; Rogers Fund, 1914*) Statue of the treasurer, Sihathor. XII Dynasty. (*The British Museum*)

68 Wooden figure of an offering bearer. From the tomb of Meketre, Thebes. XI Dynasty. (*The Metropolitan Museum of Art, Museum Excavations, 1919–20; Rogers Fund and contribution of Edward S. Harkness*)

69 Wooden model of fishing boat on the Nile. From the tomb of Meketre, Thebes. XI Dynasty. (*The Metropolitan Museum of Art, Museum Excavations, 1919–20; Rogers Fund and contribution of Edward S. Harkness*)

70 Fisherman. Detail from a wall painting in the tomb of Senet, Thebes. XII Dynasty. (*Photograph by Egyptian Expedition, The Metropolitan Museum of Art*)

71 Dancers and musicians. Detail from a wall painting in the tomb of Senet, Thebes. XII Dynasty. (*Photograph by Egyptian Expedition, The Metropolitan Museum of Art*)

72 Painting inside the coffin of Djehutynekht. From his tomb at Deir el

Bersheh. XII Dynasty. (*Courtesy, Museum of Fine Arts, Boston, Harvard University and MFA Expedition*)

74– Fowling scene. Copy of a wall paint-
75 ing in the tomb of Khnumhotep, Beni Hasan. XII Dynasty. (*The Metropolitan Museum of Art*)

76 Desert nomads. Copy of a wall painting in the tomb of Khnumhotep, Beni Hasan. XII Dynasty. (*The Metropolitan Museum of Art*)

77 Cosmetic box with mirror and stone jars. XII Dynasty. (*The Metropolitan Museum of Art*)

77 Wooden statuette of a foreign woman. From a tomb at Beni Hasan. XII Dynasty. (*Courtesy, The Royal Scottish Museum, Edinburgh*)

78 Crown of Princess Sit-Hathor-yunet. XII Dynasty. The circlet and half the tubing are reproductions of originals in the Egyptian Museum, Cairo; the other tubes are original. (*The Metropolitan Museum of Art, Contributions from Henry Walters and the Rogers Fund, 1916, and the Dodge Fund, 1931*)

79 Carved stone ointment jar in the form of kneeling girl. XII Dynasty. (*The British Museum*)

80– Jewelry of Princess Sit-Hathor-yunet,
81 XII Dynasty: gold and amethyst girdle and anklet; front and back of inlaid gold pendant. (*The Metropolitan Museum of Art, Rogers Fund and contribution from Henry Walters, 1916*)

82 Collar of beads. From the jewelry of Princess Neferwptah, daughter of King Amenemhat III. XII Dynasty. (*The Egyptian Museum, Cairo*)

83 Head of Amenhotep III. XVIII Dynasty. (*Courtesy, Museum of Fine Arts, Boston. Gift: Miss Anna D. Slocum*)

84 Granite statue of Queen Hatshepsut. From her mortuary temple at Deir el Bahri, Thebes. XVIII Dynasty. (*The Metropolitan Museum of Art, Rogers Fund, 1927*)

86 Sphinx of Queen Hatshepsut. From her temple at Deir el Bahri, Thebes. XVIII Dynasty. (*The Metropolitan Museum of Art, Rogers Fund, 1930*)

87 Temples of Queen Hatshepsut and King Mentuhotep, Deir el Bahri.

XVIII and XI Dynasties. (*Photograph: Marburg-Art Reference Bureau*)

88 Model of the mortuary temple of Queen Hatshepsut; view from the southeast. (*The Metropolitan Museum of Art*)

89 Statue of Senmut with Princess Nefrure. XVIII Dynasty. (*The Egyptian Museum, Cairo*)

92 Hall of the tomb of Menna, Thebes. XVIII Dynasty. (*Photograph by Egyptian Expedition, The Metropolitan Museum of Art*)

94– Farming scenes. Wall painting in the
95 tomb of Menna, Thebes. XVIII Dynasty. (*Photograph by Egyptian Expedition, The Metropolitan Museum of Art*)

96– Details of wall paintings in the tomb
97 of Rekhmire, Thebes. XVIII Dynasty. (*Photographs by Egyptian Expedition, The Metropolitan Museum of Art*)

98 Feasting scene. Wall painting from the tomb of Nebamun, Thebes. XVIII Dynasty. (*The British Museum*)

99 Ibex and hound. Copy of a wall painting in the tomb of Kenamun, Thebes. XVIII Dynasty. (*The Metropolitan Museum of Art*)

100– Relief carvings in the tomb of Ramose,
101 Thebes. XVIII Dynasty. (*Photographs by Egyptian Expedition, The Metropolitan Museum of Art*)

102– Relief carvings in the tomb of
103 Kheruef, Thebes. XVIII Dynasty. (*Photographs by The Epigraphic Survey, The Oriental Institute, Luxor, Egypt*)

104 Colossal statue of King Amenhotep III and Queen Tiy. XVIII Dynasty. The Egyptian Museum, Cairo. (*Photograph: Marburg-Art Reference Bureau*)

105 Syrians bringing gifts to Amenhotep III. Wall painting from the tomb of Sebenkhotep, Thebes. XVIII Dynasty. (*The British Museum*)

106 The Luxor Temple, XVIII and XIX Dynasties: view from Court of Ramesses II. (*Photograph: the author*)

107 The Luxor Temple; looking north to the pylon. (*Photograph: Courtesy of the United Arab Republic Tourist Office, New York*) .

108 The Luxor Temple: Court of Amen-

hotep III. XVIII Dynasty. (*Photograph: Art Reference Bureau*)

109 The Luxor Temple: columns in the building of Amenhotep III. XVIII Dynasty. (*Photograph: the author*)

110 Carnelian plaque from bracelet or anklet, showing Amenhotep III and his daughters. XVIII Dynasty. (*The Metropolitan Museum of Art, Carnarvon Collection, Gift of Edward S. Harkness, 1926*)

111 Head of King Akhenaten. XVIII Dynasty. (*The Metropolitan Museum of Art, Rogers Fund, 1911*)

112 King Akhenaten and his family worshiping. Relief carving from Amarna. XVIII Dynasty. The Egyptian Museum, Cairo. (*Photograph, Courtesy of The Metropolitan Museum of Art*)

114 Detail of a relief in the Amarna style. In the tomb of Ramose, Thebes. XVIII Dynasty. (*Photograph by Egyptian Expedition, The Metropolitan Museum of Art*)

115 Sculptor's trial piece. From Amarna. XVIII Dynasty. (*The Egyptian Museum, Cairo*)

116 Small unfinished statue of King Akhenaten with a child on his knee. XVIII Dynasty. (*The Egyptian Museum, Cairo*)

117 Head of Akhenaten's eldest daughter, forming the lid of a canopic jar. From the tomb of Semenkh-ka-Re, Valley of the Kings, Thebes. XVIII Dynasty. (*The Metropolitan Museum of Art, The Theodore M. Davis Collection, Bequest of Theodore M. Davis, 1915*)

118 Carved ivory panel from a box lid. From the tomb of Tutankhamen, Valley of the Kings, Thebes. XVIII Dynasty. The Egyptian Museum, Cairo. (*Photograph by Harry Burton, The Metropolitan Museum of Art*)

119 Fresco painting of ducks and papyrus. From Amarna. XVIII Dynasty. The Egyptian Museum, Cairo. (*Photograph, Courtesy of The Metropolitan Museum of Art*)

120– Treasures from the tomb of Tutank-
126 hamen, Valley of the Kings, Thebes. XVIII Dynasty. The Egyptian Museum, Cairo.
120 Back panel of the throne of Tutankhamen. (*Photograph by Harry

Burton, The Metropolitan Museum of Art*)
121 Gold mask of the mummy. (*Photograph by Harry Burton, The Metropolitan Museum of Art*)
122 Upper part of the gold coffin. (*Photograph by Harry Burton, The Metropolitan Museum of Art*)
123 Footstool of a throne. (*The Egyptian Museum, Cairo*)
124 Lower end of Tutankhamen's ceremonial walking stick. (*Photograph by Harry Burton, The Metropolitan Museum of Art*)
125 Folding stool of Nubian workmanship. (*The Egyptian Museum, Cairo*)
125–126 Details from the painted chest of Tutankhamen: Nubian battle and Syrian battle. (*Photographs by Harry Burton, The Metropolitan Museum of Art*)

127 Head of King Ramesses II. Detail of a colossal statue on the façade of the Great Temple at Abu Simbel. XIX Dynasty. (*Photograph: Courtesy of the Centre of Documentation and Studies on Ancient Egypt, Cairo*)

128– Relief carvings on the north wall of
129 the Hypostyle Hall. Temple of Amon, Karnak. XIX Dynasty.
128 Battle at Kadesh. (*Photograph: the author*)
129 Herdsman fleeing from the battle at Kadesh. Detail of relief on page 128. (*Photograph by The Epigraphic Survey, The Oriental Institute, Luxor, Egypt*) King Seti I with prisoners of war. (*Photograph: the author*)

130 Central aisle of the Hypostyle Hall, Temple of Amon, Karnak. XIX Dynasty. (*Photograph: Marburg-Art Reference Bureau*)

131 Sacred bark of Amon carried in procession. Relief in the Hypostyle Hall, Karnak. XIX Dynasty. (*Photograph: the author*)

132 King Ramesses II receiving the emblems of office from the god Amon. Relief in the Hypostyle Hall, Karnak. XIX Dynasty. (*Photograph: the author*)

133 The Great Temple, Abu Simbel (on its original site). XIX Dynasty. (*Photograph: Courtesy of the Centre of Documentation and Studies on Ancient Egypt, Cairo*)

134 Colossal statue of King Ramesses II

PAGE

on the façade of the Great Temple, Abu Simbel. XIX Dynasty. (*Photograph: Courtesy of the Centre of Documentation and Studies on Ancient Egypt, Cairo*)

135 Façade of the Temple of Hathor, Abu Simbel. XIX Dynasty. (*Photograph: Marburg-Art Reference Bureau*)
Hittite and Syrian prisoners. Carvings on the base of one of the colossal statues of Ramesses II on the façade of the Great Temple, Abu Simbel. XIX Dynasty. (*Photographs: the author*)

136 Hall of the Great Temple, Abu Simbel. XIX Dynasty. (*Photograph: Marburg-Art Reference Bureau*)

138– The Battle of Kadesh. Relief carving
139 in the Ramasseum (mortuary temple of Ramesses II), Thebes. XIX Dynasty. (*Photograph by The Epigraphic Survey, The Oriental Institute, Luxor, Egypt*)

140 Pylon of the Temple of Ramesses III at Medinet Habu, Thebes. XX Dynasty. (*Photograph: Marburg-Art Reference Bureau*)

141 Hunting scenes. Relief carving on the back of the pylon, Temple of Ramesses III, Medinet Habu. XX Dynasty. (*Photograph by Egyptian Expedition, The Metropolitan Museum of Art*)

142 Bull hunt. Detail of the lower section of the relief shown on page 141. (*Photograph by Egyptian Expedition, The Metropolitan Museum of Art*)

143 Restored foundations of the palace at Medinet Habu. (*Photograph: the author*)

144 Foundations of the village of the craftsmen, Deir el Medineh, Thebes. (*Photograph: the author*)

145 Flake of limestone with sketch of a hunting scene. From a tomb at Deir el Medineh. (*The Egyptian Museum, Cairo*)

146 Draftsman's practice board with hieroglyphs and figure of a king. XVIII–XXI Dynasty. (*The British Museum*)

147 Painted ceiling of the burial chamber in the tomb of Seti I, Valley of the Kings, Thebes. XIX Dynasty. (*Photograph: Marburg-Art Reference Bureau*)

148 The weighing of the heart. From the papyrus of Hunefer. XIX Dynasty. (*The British Museum*)

PAGE

149 The dead man before Osiris. From the Book of the Dead of the scribe Ani. (*The British Museum*)

150 Flake of limestone with sketch of cat and geese. From a tomb at Deir el Medineh. (*The Egyptian Museum, Cairo*)

151 Painted tomb of Sennedjem, Deir el Medineh, Thebes. XIX Dynasty. (*Photograph by Egyptian Expedition, The Metropolitan Museum of Art*)

152 Metalworkers. Detail from a wall painting in the tomb of Rekhmire, Thebes. XVIII Dynasty. (*Photograph by Egyptian Expedition, The Metropolitan Museum of Art*)

Drawings

HALF TITLE AND PAGE 5 Singer and flute-player; singer and harpist. Details of a relief carving from a tomb at Sakkara. V Dynasty. The Egyptian Museum, Cairo.

PAGE

17 Desert animals. Detail of relief carving on the "Hunter's Palette." Predynastic Period. The British Museum.

23 Crowns of the kings of Egypt: White Crown of Upper Egypt; Red Crown of Lower Egypt; Double Crown of the Two Lands.

25 Symbols representing the union of the Two Lands:
Above "The Two Ladies"—the vulture goddess Nekhbet of the south and the cobra goddess Wadjet of the north.
Below The sedge plant of the south and the bee of the north.

26 Picture writing, representing a bee, a bull and a man.

27 The word "pyramid" in hieroglyphs.

28 *Above* Seal in the shape of scarab beetle. XVIII Dynasty. The Metropolitan Museum of Art.
Below "The Two Ladies"—vulture and cobra goddesses.

30 *Top left* Thoth, god of scribes.
Top right Ibis, hoopoe and herons in a papyrus marsh. Detail of a relief in a royal tomb. V Dynasty. The Egyptian Museum, Cairo.
Bottom Alabaster figure of a baboon. I Dynasty. The Berlin Museum.

158

PAGE

34 *Top* "Horus-name" of King Zoser.*
   Bottom *Mastaba* tomb.

35 Plan of the Step Pyramid and courtyard, Sakkara.

36 *Top* Papyrus-stem column from the "Northern Building" in the courtyard of the Step Pyramid, Sakkara. III Dynasty.
   Bottom Stone vase from chamber under the Step Pyramid. III Dynasty.

37 King Zoser performing a religious ceremony. From a relief carving under the Step Pyramid. III Dynasty.

41 Cartouche with the name of King Khufu, as "King of Upper and Lower Egypt."†

43 Section of the Pyramid of Khufu. Plan of Pyramids, Temples and Tombs at Giza.

45 Cartouche with the name of King Khafre.

46 Plan of Khafre's Valley Temple.

49 Cartouche with the name of King Menkaure.

53 *Top* Harvest scene
   Bottom Roping cattle. Both from reliefs in the tomb of Mereruka, Sakkara. VI Dynasty.

60 Limestone statuette of brewer straining beer. From a tomb at Sakkara. V Dynasty. The Egyptian Museum, Cairo.

61 Scribe at work. Detail of a relief carving from a tomb at Giza. IV Dynasty. The Museum of Fine Arts, Boston.

64 Cartouches with two royal names of King Mentuhotep II, as "King of Upper and Lower Egypt" and "Son of Re."

65 *Top* Reconstruction of Mentuhotep's temple at Deir el Bahri, Thebes.
   Bottom Statuette of a man, inscribed with a prayer to the god Ptah for the man's soul. XII Dynasty. The Metropolitan Museum of Art.

66 Cartouches with two royal names of King Senwosret III.

73 Offering bearers. Detail from the painted coffin of Djehuty-nekht. XII

Dynasty. The Museum of Fine Arts, Boston.

74 Palette of King Narmer (front). I Dynasty. The Egyptian Museum, Cairo.

75 Seated figure of the priest Ra-hetep. Detail of a relief from his tomb at Meidum. IV Dynasty. The British Museum.

79 Toilet of a queen. From relief carving on the coffin of Queen Kawit. XI Dynasty. The Egyptian Museum, Cairo.

81 Collar of beads. From painting on the coffin of Djehuty-nekht. XII Dynasty.

85 Cartouches with two royal names of Queen Hatshepsut.

86 Sistrum (musical instrument used in religious processions).

88– Details from reliefs in the Temple of
91 Hatshepsut, Deir el Bahri, Thebes:
   88 Ruler of Punt and his wife.
   89 House on stilts in the Land of Punt.
   90–91 *Top* Produce of Punt brought to the Egyptians.
   90 *Bottom* Departure of the Egyptian ships.

93 Plan of a typical rock-cut tomb-chapel at Thebes.

106 Plan of the Luxor Temple.

109 Decorated oxen for sacrifice. Detail from reliefs of the Opet procession in the Luxor Temple (west wall of the Court of Ramesses II). XIX Dynasty.

110 Cartouches with two royal names of King Amenhotep III.

113 Bowing figure. Detail from relief carving in Amarna style in the tomb of Ramose, Thebes. XVIII Dynasty.

114 Cartouches with two royal names of King Akhenaten.

119 Ivory statuette of gazelle. XVIII Dynasty. The Metropolitan Museum of Art.

121 Cartouche of King Tutankhamen.

124 Painted chest of Tutankhamen. XVIII Dynasty. The Egyptian Museum, Cairo.

129 Cartouches with two royal names of King Seti I.

* In the First, Second and Third Dynasties the principal name of the king was his "Horus-name." The hieroglyphs of the name were enclosed in a rectangular frame with the Horus falcon on the top (as shown in the photograph of the stele of King Uadji on page 29).

† From the Fourth Dynasty onward, the king usually had five names. The two most commonly used were enclosed in oval cartouches and preceded by the royal titles:
   "King of Upper and Lower Egypt" and "Son of Re" .

PAGE

131 Plan of the Temple of Amon, Karnak, in the time of Ramesses II.

132 Cartouches with two royal names of King Ramesses II.

137 The King smiting enemy prisoners: *Left* King Narmer. From the Palette of King Narmer. I Dynasty. The Egyptian Museum, Cairo. *Right* King Ramesses II. From a relief in the hall of the Great Temple, Abu Simbel. XIX Dynasty.

140 Cartouches with two royal names of King Ramesses III.

PAGE

143 Wrestlers. From a relief in the first courtyard of the Temple of Ramesses III, Medinet Habu, Thebes. XX Dynasty.

144 Tools of the scribe: palettes and rush pens.

145 Rearing serpent. Detail from decorations of the tomb of King Seti I, Valley of the Kings, Thebes. XIX Dynasty.

153 The Ankh, sign of life, held in the hand of King Amenhotep III. Detail of relief carving in the tomb of Kheruef, Thebes, XVIII Dynasty.

Books for Further Reading

Aldred, Cyril. *The Development of Ancient Egyptian Art*. London: Alec Tiranti, 1965.

————. *The Egyptians*. New York: Frederick A. Praeger *(Ancient Peoples and Places)*, 1963.

The British Museum. *Introductory Guide to the Egyptian Collections*. London: The Trustees of the British Museum, 1964.

Desroches-Noblecourt, Christiane. *Tutankhamen*. Greenwich, Connecticut: New York Graphic Society, 1963.

Dunham, Dows. *The Egyptian Department and Its Excavations*. Boston: Museum of Fine Arts, 1958.

Edwards, I. E. S. *The Pyramids of Egypt*. Harmondsworth, England: Penguin Books, rev. ed. 1961.

Emery, W. B. *Archaic Egypt*. Harmondsworth, England: Penguin Books, 1961.

Fakhry, Ahmed. *The Pyramids*. Chicago: University of Chicago Press, 1961.

Hayes, William C. *The Scepter of Egypt,* 2 vols. New York: Metropolitan Museum of Art, 1953, 1959.

Nims, Charles F. *Thebes of the Pharaohs*. New York: Stein & Day, 1965.

Rachewiltz, Boris de. *An Introduction to Egyptian Art*. London: Spring Books, 1966.

Riefstahl, Elizabeth. *Thebes in the Time of Amenhotep III*. Norman, Oklahoma: University of Oklahoma Press *(The Centers of Civilization Series)*, 1964.

Smith, William Stevenson. *Ancient Egypt*. Boston: Museum of Fine Arts, 1960.

Steindorff, George and Seele, Keith C. *When Egypt Ruled the East*. Chicago: University of Chicago Press (Phoenix Books), 1963.

Ward, William A. *The Spirit of Ancient Egypt*. Beirut, Lebanon: Khayats, 1965.

Wilson, John A. *The Culture of Ancient Egypt*. Chicago: University of Chicago Press (Phoenix Books), 1956.